# Philosophy of Education

## An Introduction

# T. W. Moore

INTERNATIONAL LIBRARY OF
THE PHILOSOPHY OF EDUCATION
General Editor R.S. Peters

*A Selection of Books in the*
**International Library of Philosophy of Education**

*****Education and the Development of Reason**
*Edited by R. F. Dearden, P. H. Hirst and R. S. Peters*
Also available in three paperback volumes

†**Educational Judgments**
*Edited by James F. Doyle*

†**Ethics and Educational Policy**
*Edited by Kenneth A. Strike and Kieran Egan*

†**Experience and the Growth of Understanding**
*D. W. Hamlyn*

†**Knowledge and the Curriculum**
A Collection of Philosophical Papers
*Paul H. Hirst*

*****Preface to the Philosophy of Education**
*John Wilson*

*Also available in paperback
†Available in paperback only

**Routledge & Kegan Paul**

International
Library of the
Philosophy of
Education

**Philosophy of education:
an introduction**

International
Library of the
Philosophy of
Education

General Editor

R. S. Peters

Professor of Philosophy of Education
Institute of Education
University of London

# Philosophy of education:
## an introduction

## T. W. Moore
**Institute of Education**
**University of London**

## Routledge & Kegan Paul
### London and New York

First published in 1982
by Routledge & Kegan Paul Ltd
11 New Fetter Lane, London EC4P 4EE
Published in the USA by
Routledge and Kegan Paul Inc.
in association with Methuen Inc.
29 West 35th Street, New York, NY10001.
Set in Baskerville by
Donald Typesetting, Bristol
and printed in Great Britain by
T. J. Press (Padstow) Ltd
Padstow, Cornwall

Reprinted 1986

Library of Congress Cataloging in Publication Data

Moore, T. W.
Philosophy of education.
(International library of the philosophy of
education)
Bibliography: p.
Includes index.
1. Education — Philosophy. I. Title. II. Series.
LB1025.2.M57      370'.1      82-3670

ISBN 0 7100 9192 3              AACR2

# Contents

# Contents

# General editor's note

There is a growing interest in philosophy of education amongst students of philosophy as well as amongst those who are more specifically and practically concerned with educational problems. Philosophers, of course, from the time of Plato onwards, have taken an interest in education and have dealt with education in the context of wider concerns about knowledge and the good life. But it is only quite recently in this country that philosophy of education has come to be conceived of as a specific branch of philosophy like the philosophy of science or political philosophy.

To call philosophy of education a specific branch of philosophy is not, however, to suggest that it is a distinct branch in the sense that it could exist apart from established branches of philosophy such as epistemology, ethics and philosophy of mind. It would be more appropriate to conceive of it as drawing on established branches of philosophy and bringing them together in ways which are relevant to educational issues. In this respect the analogy with political philosophy would be a good one. Thus use can often be made of work that already exists in philosophy. In tackling, for instance, issues such as the rights of parents and children, punishment in schools, and the authority of the teacher, it is possible to draw on and develop work already done by philosophers on 'rights', 'punishment', and 'authority'. In other cases, however, no systematic work exists in the relevant branches of philosophy—e.g. on concepts such as 'education', 'teaching', 'learning', 'indoctrination'. So philosophers of education have had to break new ground—in these cases in the philosophy of mind. Work on educational issues can also bring to life and throw new light on long-standing problems in philosophy. Concentration, for instance, on the particular predicament of children can throw new light on problems of punishment and responsibility. G.E. Moore's old worries about what sorts of things are good in themselves can be brought to life by urgent questions about the justification of the curriculum in schools.

There is a danger in philosophy of education, as in any other applied field, of polarisation to one of two extremes. The work could be practically relevant but philosophically feeble; or it could be philosophically sophisticated but remote from practical problems. The aim of the new International Library of the Philosophy of Education is to build up a body of fundamental work in this area which is both practically relevant and philosophically competent. For unless it achieves both types of objective it will fail to satisfy those for whom it is intended and fall short of the conception of philosophy of education which the International Library is meant to embody.

The International Library has, for a long time, been in need of a suitable introduction which would help students to find their way about its other volumes. Mr Moore has supplied just what is required: an introduction that is clear and balanced with further readings to guide students who wish to go more deeply into the topics he discusses.

The book opens with an account of the change, both in philosophy and philosophy of education, during the past thirty years. It attempts to demarcate the position of philosophy of education both in relation to philosophy and to educational theory and practice. Within educational theory there is a discussion of the time-honoured topic of aims of education, which is illustrated by the theories of writers such as Helvetius and Skinner which depended on a mechanical view of human nature and those of Froebel and Dewey which depended on an organic view. Throughout Mr Moore stresses that philosophy of education is theory-laden.

After dealing with these general matters, Mr Moore passes to the more practical level of the curriculum. The nature of knowledge is discussed and its relation to the curriculum. The implications for the curriculum of Utilitarianism, Professor Hirst's 'forms of knowledge' and Michael Oakeshott's 'heritage' view are briefly and critically sketched. Mr Moore stresses the importance of making clear whether just knowledge or the *worth* of knowledge is under consideration. The distinctions between 'teaching', 'educating', and 'in-doctrination' are examined, as well as the progressive and traditional approaches to teaching. Discipline and punishment are distinguished from each other, and their connections with authority explored. Throughout Mr Moore takes a balanced position between progressive and traditional theories.

In dealing with the connection, or lack of it, between morals and religion on the one hand and education on the other, Mr Moore stresses the contingency of the relationship. Though sympathetic to the teaching of morality in schools, and tolerant of the teaching of religion, he insists that this is a matter of moral decision, not of conceptual necessity. He is also opposed to using other subjects, such as history and literature, to teach moral beliefs or religious doctrines. He finally outlines the social setting of education. Questions are raised about equality, freedom, and democracy in education. A sharp distinction is made between equalitarianism and justice; the complications of freedom in education are explored; and the paternalistic type of 'people's democracy' of the East is distinguished from Western democracy. In dealing with democracy in the school Mr Moore examines how far its unavoidable paternalism can be modified to meet democratic demands.

This concise introduction to philosophy of education is readable, succinct, and informative. It should be of great help to teachers, and any one interested in philosophy of education, to find their way into the considerable literature that now exists in this branch of educational studies.

R.S.P.

# Acknowledgments

My thanks are due to my colleagues at the London Institute of Education who helped me with this book. Reynold Jones read the first draft and discussed it with me. Richard Peters read the completed work and, in commenting on it, gave liberally of his knowledge and experience. The imperfections in the book which remain are all my own.

I should like here to acknowledge my debt to the students whom I have taught over many years at the Institute, and from whom I am inclined to think that I have received as much as I ever gave. This book is to a great extent the result of the very stimulating encounters between us.

# Philosophy and philosophy of education   1

## 1 Introduction

This book sets out to give a brief and elementary introduction to philosophy of education, a specialised branch
of philosophy. A preliminary move must be to say
something about the two, about what kind of study
philosophy is and about what philosophers of education
generally are trying to do. Unfortunately there are no
simple and uncontentious answers to questions which are
bound to be asked here. Philosophers themselves are forever debating what philosophy is and what sort of
enquiries philosophers pursue, and apart from a general
agreement that philosophy tries to get at the truth on
certain important questions by rational means, there is
little consensus about what philosophers are doing or
ought to be doing. This is true also of philosophers of
education, amongst whom there is quite considerable
diversity of opinion about what exactly their task is or
ought to be. What follows is therefore offered with
some caution. It tries to present a particular view of the
nature and role of philosophy of education and it is
inevitable that the conclusions given will not all be
acceptable to everyone who works in this field. Nevertheless, given this reservation it is hoped that there will
be substance enough to enable the newcomer to the
subject to follow and perhaps take part in the ongoing

debate about its scope and its role in educational thinking.

This chaper is concerned mainly with the relationship which exists between what may be called general philosophy, philosophy of education and educational theory.

## 2 Philosophy and philosophy of education

Philosophy of education is connected with general philosophy partly by its purposes but more directly by its methods. To explain this we need to look at the nature of philosophy as an enterprise. In the past it was thought to be the philosopher's job to give a comprehensive and rational account of the nature of reality and of man's place in the scheme of things, and to deal with issues like the existence of God, the immortality of the soul and the purpose of the universe. Philosophy conducted in this way and to this end is known as metaphysics and from Plato's day until comparatively recently metaphysics in one form or another has been the main area of traditional philosophical activity. Plato, Aristotle, Descartes, Spinoza and Hegel, for example, were to a large extent occupied with giving something like an overall picture of reality supported by arguments of a rational kind. The trouble with this kind of philosophy, however, was that each philosopher gave a different account and no one account was found to be generally satisfactory. After more than two thousand years of metaphysical speculation questions about the true nature of reality, the existence of God, the nature of man and his soul, and the purpose of the universe are still asked and still call for a generally acceptable answer.

This persistence of problems in philosophy has been seen as being in great contrast to the history of problems encountered in science. It was noted that whereas scientists tended to solve their problems philosophers rarely if ever solved theirs. Philosophers were still dealing with the metaphysical problems raised by Plato. So sometime during the first third of the present century a conviction grew that perhaps the whole enterprise was misconceived. Scientists, it came to be said, solved their problems because they had genuine problems to solve and effective methods to solve them. Philosophers, puzzled by metaphysical questions, did not solve their problems because their problems were not really problems at all. They were pseudo-problems generated usually by a misuse of language. This conviction led to a radical rethinking about the proper role and methods of philosophical enquiry.

It is not easy to give brief and convincing examples to illustrate what was called the 'revolution in philosophy' initiated by philosophers like G.E. Moore and Ludwig Wittgenstein, and their disciples, but two such examples may help. Metaphysicians like Descartes had supposed that since the word 'body' was the name of a substantial material entity, the associated word 'mind' must also be the name of an entity, a substance, but of a non-material kind. This assumption led to a particularly intractable philosophical problem: how does a non-material substance interact with and affect a material one, and vice versa? Granted the initial assumption the supposed interaction was a great mystery and a satisfactory explanation of it elusive. The new approach to philosophy, which saw philosophical problems as arising from the misuse of language, made it seem

3

possible to account for and get rid of problems of the 'mind-body' sort. It was, for example, maintained by Gilbert Ryle [22] that if we abandon the assumption that for a word to be meaningful there must be some substantial entity for it to refer to, the mind–body problem no longer seems intractable. The term 'mind', Ryle argued, is not the name of a non–material entity. Indeed it is not the name of a substantial entity at all and so the problem of how mind interacts with body is not a genuine problem. To talk of the mind, Ryle maintained, is to talk about certain kinds of behaviour. 'Mind' is not the name of a thing or a substance but of a complicated set of bodily functions carried out in certain characteristic ways. If this account is accepted the long-standing metaphysical 'mind-body' problem vanishes. The mind doesn't interact with the body; it is simply a function of the body. Thus the problem of interaction is not solved so much as dissolved; it ceases to exist.

Again, questions about the possible 'purpose' of the universe presented metaphysicians with considerable difficulties. How could one ever decide what the purpose of the universe was, supposing it to have one? Metaphysicians' answers to this question were generally unsatisfactory since they seemed always to beg important questions, like that of the existence of God. Moreover there was no conclusive way of telling whether such answers as were given were true or false. Faced with such difficulties philosophers now tried not to solve the problem but to dissolve it. One way of doing this was to point out that whilst it is appropriate to ask the purpose of things, tools, gadgets and the like, which exist *within* the universe, it doesn't make sense to ask the same question of the whole, of the universe itself

The universe is, by definition, 'all there is', and so what possible external purpose could it serve? The universe is an end in itself. The problem about what other end it serves, what its purpose is, is merely a pseudo-problem arising from the erroneous assumption that it makes sense to ask questions about the whole which are only appropriately asked of the parts. Once this is understood the problem ceases to be a problem. This kind of philosophising had for its purpose a kind of intellectual therapy, a ridding of the mind of unnecessary and self-inflicted problems.

It is not claimed here that these examples give unexceptionable answers to the problems referred to. They are given to show the shift in emphasis in philosophy, from attempts to deal with substantial issues, about what exists or has purposes, to an examination of the language in which the supposed problems are stated. Philosophy, it was now said, is strictly a 'higher-order' activity dealing with linguistic and conceptual issues, with the 'concept of mind' or the 'concept of purpose', rather than with minds or purposes as such, and dealing with problems which arise wholly or largely from linguistic or conceptual confusions. Philosophy came increasingly to be thought of as the analysis and clarification of concepts used in other areas. Philosophy, it was maintained, has no distinctive subject-matter of its own. It is a general mode of enquiry, about the concepts and theories presupposed in other disciplines, science, for example, or mathematics, history, law, or religion, and is concerned, moreover, with the arguments and justifications found in those theories. Its aim is to bring clarity to the concepts, to test the coherence of the theories, and to serve the therapeutic purpose of dissolving those problems which persist only because of linguistic confusions. This view of philosophy in general is a matter of debate which will not be pursued here. What will be maintained throughout this book is that philosophy as such is parasitic on theory and that philosophy of education is a higher-order activity which has for its host the theory and practice of education.

A word of caution is needed here. Whilst it is true that some contemporary philosophy and certainly much philosophy engaged in over the past thirty years or so has been concerned with the identification and dissolution of pseudo-problems, it cannot be claimed that philosophy of education has made or has needed to make much headway in this direction. The problems thrown up by education are not usually problems arising from conceptual confusion, but are real substantial problems arising out of practice. These problems need to be solved rather than dissolved. Philosophers of education are not normally preoccupied with metaphysical confusions. They certainly engage in a higher-order activity but their interest is with conceptual clarity as a preliminary to the justification of educational theory and practice. The preoccupation with clarity involves them in philosophical analysis, the analysis of concepts; the concern with the need for justification requires them to scrutinise the various theories of education which have been offered. This is why it was said earlier that philosophy of education is connected with general philosophy more directly by its methods than by its therapeutic purposes. Philosophy of education focuses on the language of educational theory and practice. The nature of these areas and the relationship between them now need to be examined.

## 3 The nature of educational theory

Philosophers of education, then, are concerned with a scrutiny of what is said about education by those who practise it and by those who theorise about it. We may regard the complicated phenomena of education as a group of activities going on at various logical levels, 'logical' in the sense that each higher level arises out of and is dependent on the one below it. The lowest level is the level of educational practice at which activities like teaching, instructing, motivating pupils, advising them, and correcting their work are carried on. Those engaged at this level, teachers mainly, will employ a language specifically adapted to deal with their work and they will use a specific conceptual apparatus when they discuss what they are doing. They will talk about 'teaching', 'learning', 'knowledge', 'experience' . . . an indefinite number of such topics, with an indefinite number of associated concepts. These activities and these concepts are basic. Unless educational activities were carried on and talked about there would be no subject matter for higher-order activities to work on. Arising out of these basic ground-floor activities is another activity, educational theorising, the first of these higher-order concerns. The result of educational theorising is educational theory, or more accurately, educational theories.[12] The connection between practice and theory is complicated and will be looked at later in this chapter. Here it will be sufficient to say that educational theorising may be one or other of two kinds. The theorist may be making a general point *about* education. He may say, for example, that education is the most effective way, or the only way, of socialising the young, of converting them from human animals into human beings, or of enabling them to realise their intellectual and moral potentialities. Or he may say that education is the best way to establish a sense of social solidarity, by giving everyone a common cultural background. It is not important here whether or not such contentions are true. It is important to notice that they *could* be true or false. It may well be true that education of the formal kind is an effective way of socialising the young or of securing social cohesion. Whether it is so or not is a matter of fact and the way to find out is to look at education in practice and see what happens. In other words, theories of this kind are descriptive theories, purporting to give a correct account of what education, as a matter of fact, does. Such theories stand or fall according to the way the world happens to be. They belong to the social sciences, to descriptive sociology.

The other kind of educational theory is one which does not set out, primarily at least, to give a description of the role or function of education but rather to give advice or recommendations about what those engaged in educational practice *ought* to be doing. Such theories are 'practical' theories, giving reasoned prescriptions for action. Theories of this kind exhibit a wide variety, in scope, content and complexity. Some of them are fairly limited in character, such as the theory that teachers should make sure that any new material introduced to the pupil should be linked to what he knows already, or that a child should not be told a fact before he has had a chance to find it out for himself. Limited theories like this may perhaps be better called theories of teaching, or pedagogical theories. Other theories of this kind are wider in scope and more complex, such as the theory that education ought to promote the development of the innate potentialities of the pupil, or that it ought to prepare him for work, or to be a good citizen or a good democrat. Theories like these may be called 'general theories of education' in that they give comprehensive prescriptions, recommending the production of a particular type of person and, very often, a specific type of society. These overall types of educational theory are often met with in the writings of those who for other reasons are known as philosophers. Plato, for instance, gives a general theory of education in the dialogue known as *The Republic*, in which his aim is to recommend a certain type of man as worthy to be the ruler of a distinctive type of society. Rousseau gives a general theory of education in *Emile*. Others are given in Froebel's *The Education of Man*, in James Mill's 'Essay on Education', and Dewey's *Democracy and Education*. In each case the theory involves a set of prescriptions addressed to those engaged in the practice of education, and in most cases, if not in all, the theory is meant to serve an external end, to prescribe a political, social or religious way of life. General theories of education are very often influential essays in propaganda.

Two further points need to be made here about these general, prescriptive theories. First, it must be recognised that, unlike theories *about* education, they do not belong to the social sciences. They are not meant to be descriptions of what actually goes on in the world, but are recommendations about what *ought* to be done. As such they involve a deliberate commitment on the part of the theorist, an assumption of some end which he considers ought to be adopted and worked for. The

9

recommendations which constitute the conclusions set out in the theory presuppose a major value component, the notion of an 'educated man'. This value commitment means that theories of this kind cannot be verified or validated in the way that scientific, descriptive theories may be. Whereas a scientist is committed only to the formal assumption that the truth is worth having but not to any prior notion about what that truth should be, an educational theorist commits himself initially to the conviction that a certain substantial state of affairs is desirable, that a certain type of individual should exist. So whilst a scientific theory may be established or rejected simply by checking it against the facts of the empirical world, the validation of a prescriptive theory demands a more complex and piecemeal approach, involving both an appeal to empirical evidence and a justification of a substantial value judgement.

The second point is that such general theories are sometimes known as 'philosophies of education', so that one reads of Plato's, or Froebel's, or Dewey's 'philosophy of education'. This book takes the view that to call them such is misleading. Not all that is written by philosophers qualifies as philosophy, and these comprehensive practical theories of education are not themselves philosophical products. They are general theories *of* education offered by philosophers. They may be closely connected with philosophy of education but the connection is not that of equivalence or identity. What the connection is, in fact, now needs to be looked at.

## 4 Educational theory and educational practice

We may do this by bringing together points made in the first two sections of this chapter to show the role and function of philosophy of education. In section 1 it was said that contemporary philosophy tends now to be seen as a higher-order activity which deals with conceptual and linguistic problems arising out of ground-floor activities like science, mathematics and history, using the content of these disciplines as subject matter. In section 2 it was maintained that education itself is a first-order activity, concerned with teaching and developing the young. Education has its own immediate higher-order activity, educational theorising, the making of theories about education and theories of education. The further point was made that philosophy of education is another higher-order activity parasitic upon the practice and theory of education. It is not the same thing as educational theory, but it takes theory as its main subject matter. This contention must now be dealt with in more detail.

Teachers engage themselves professionally in educational activities, ground-floor activities of a certain kind. They teach in various ways: they set tasks for pupils, they try to motivate pupils, to help them, to control their performances, and to improve their understanding and skills. In doing all this they necessarily act on theories of a practical kind. A practical theory involves a commitment to some end thought worth accomplishing, and everything a teacher does in his professional work involves such a commitment, together with a recognition that certain measures are necessary to bring about that end. Even mundane, everyday classroom activities like asking children to be quiet, to open their books and to write in them are based on theories, limited theories admittedly, but theories nonetheless. It is held as a theory that if you want pupils to hear what you say you must see to it that they are reasonably quiet; that if the teacher wants them to write something he must see that they have writing materials. If the teacher allows children to work in groups, this follows from a theory about the best way to achieve his educational ends; if he organises their work on the basis of individual discovery, this too follows from a theory. All practice is theory-loaded and educational theory is logically prior to educational practice. Unless what is done is done according to some theory, bearing in mind some desirable end to be achieved and the means to achieve it, it is not practice at all, merely random behaviour. What applies to everyday classroom affairs applies to the general stance a teacher takes up about his work. If he deliberately allows the children the maximum amount of freedom in what they do, he does so according to some libertarian theory; if his teaching is didactic and authoritarian, this once again follows from a theory about the way in which the desired educational end is best achieved. More generally still, if his teaching aims at producing well-integrated personalities, or democratic citizens or dedicated communists or dedicated Christians, he is in each case acting on a theory. It is well worth insisting on this priority of theory to practice, since it is often thought to be the other way round, that theory always follows on practice. The fact is that what is codified in theoretical treatises are either those theories which have already been put into practice, or those which it is thought ought to be so. Theories may be amended or refined as a result of putting them into practice, but in no way does practice precede some theory. This is true of education as of practice generally. Behind all educational practice lies a theory of some kind.

Now, what can be put into practice can be put into words and talked about. So in addition to the actual practices of the classroom there is talk about what is done there and what ought to be done there. This is educational discourse which, in so far as it is serious, will consist partly of descriptions of what is being done, what is being taught and how, what results are being obtained, and partly of recommendations about what ought to be done, with arguments to back up these recommendations. Educational discourse will consist largely of educational theory more or less informally expressed. At the classroom or staffroom level the theories will be at their most informal, often more implied than explicit, and will usually only be made explicit when assertions or recommendations are challenged. At educational conferences theory may well be more detailed, structured and explicit. When the discourse comes to be formally set down, in books, the theories will be at their most explicit, with serious attempts at a convincing rationale. At both the practical and theoretical levels the specific conceptual apparatus will be employed. Teachers talking amongst themselves about their work and educational theorists making reasoned recommendations for practice will inevitably make use of concepts like 'education', 'teaching', 'knowledge', 'the curriculum', 'authority', 'equal opportunity', and 'punishment', amongst others. And in so far as there is explicit theorising about educa-

tion there will be argument and attempts at justification, since prescriptive educational theory is never
simply a matter of assertion. Theory will involve
recommendations backed up by reasons, which may be
appropriate or not, relevant or not, adequate or not.

## 5 Philosophy of education

This body of educational discourse is subject matter for
the philosopher of education. His concern with it will be
twofold. He will be interested in the conceptual
apparatus employed. He will want to examine the major
concepts used by practising teachers and theorists to see
what exactly is being said by this kind of language.
What, he will ask, does 'education' involve? What
exactly is 'teaching'? What has to be the case before anyone can properly be said to 'know' anything? What
criteria have to be satisfied before what a teacher does
can truly be characterised as 'punishing'? What is meant
by saying that all children ought to be given 'equal
opportunities'? What is meant by 'freedom' in an educational context? Questions like these and the answers to
them involve the philosopher in philosophical analysis
in trying to work out the criteria for the correct use of
these terms. This activity of analysis is important
perhaps in its own right, but certainly so as a preliminary to the second of the philosopher's interests, the
examination of educational theory. For educational
discourse is to a large extent a matter of educational
theory and theories need to be scrutinised to see
whether they are well founded or not. The philosopher
is concerned with the acceptability of educational
theory and a practical prerequisite of any enquiry into

the credentials of a theory is that the terms used in it should be made as clear as possible. Conceptual analysis is thus the first step in the scrutiny. Then comes the examination of the theory itself, of its internal coherence, its conformity with what is known about human nature, its conformity with accepted moral convictions and its general practicability. Confronted with a general theory of education the philosopher will ask: what is being recommended here? and: will it do?

This scrutiny may be carried out in more than one way. One way would be to take a historical approach and deal with the more important theories of education in turn, beginning with Plato and working through those of, say, Rousseau, Mill, Froebel and Spencer, and ending with more or less modern theorists like Dewey. This would require an examination of the various assumptions made in each case, assumptions about what was to count as an educated man, about human nature, about the nature of knowledge and methods, testing each assumption, and the argument as a whole, to see how far what was being said could be rationally maintained. Another way, which will be followed in the remainder of this book, is to look at educational theory in terms of major topics of interest which have emerged. In the past, and still today, those who have been concerned with education have put forward a number of views and have adopted a wide range of positions respecting educational practice. These views have ranged from more or less conventional and unreflecting comments on schooling to detailed accounts of the roles and functions of education in society. They have attempted answers to questions like: what is education? What is the purpose of it? What should be taught? Why should some subjects be taught and not others? How should pupils be taught? How should they be disciplined and controlled? Who should be educated and how should educational advantages be distributed? In other words they try to answer questions about the curriculum, about worthwhile knowledge, about teaching methods, about social considerations like the need for equality, freedom, authority and democracy in education. These answers have been embodied in educational theories, either explicit or implicit in practice. Questions like these and the answers to them have interested not only the great historical theorists like Plato and Rousseau, but also many of those engaged in everyday educational affairs. The questions are important questions and the answers to them no less so, since the way in which such questions are answered will to a large extent determine what is done in practice and this in turn will have social and other consequences of a far-reaching kind. Philosophy of education, which is concerned with the theories on which such positions are grounded, can be most usefully engaged in a critical scrutiny of these views and answers. It is central to the thesis of this book that practice is theory-loaded. If this is correct, then the need for such a scrutiny is obvious. Inadequate theory will lead to inadequate practice and inadequate practice to inadequately educated people. Philosophy of education thus has an important social function quite apart from any intrinsic interest it may have.

## 6 Conclusion

The introduction to this chapter sketched in a view of philosophy which sees it as a higher-order activity aimed at ridding the mind of problems which exist only as the result of conceptual or linguistic confusions. It is not proposed here to defend this view of philosophy or to suggest that this is the only way in which philosophy may be understood. Indeed, as was indicated earlier, it is by no means clear that this view explains adequately all that a philosopher of education tries to do, since most of the problems that concern him do not arise from linguistic confusion but are more often problems about justification. The sketch was given simply to show an analogous shift in 'educational philosophy'. What usually went under this heading in the past were comprehensive theories of education, general theories which tried to deal with education in something like the way in which metaphysicians dealt with reality. These historical general theories often had great merits and they are still worthy of study, but they also had considerable shortcomings, some of which will be referred to in the next chapter. One major disadvantage which beset them was that they were often grounded on assumptions not generally acceptable, often adopted unargued and seldom based on systematic research. Nowadays this kind of educational philosophy has largely been replaced by a view which tends to distinguish between educational theory and philosophy of education and which holds the philosopher's task not to be that of elaborating general theories but rather that of analysis and criticism. Thus understood philosophy of education may lack the glamour attached to the provision of large-scale educational recommendations and to the philosophy which deals with the giant confusions of metaphysics. Philosophers of education are rarely able to get rid of an educational problem by dissolving it.

Nevertheless, the patient examination of the conceptual apparatus of educational discourse and the painstaking enquiry into the credentials of educational theorising, past and present, make up in utility for what they may lack in intellectual excitement.

Two further points may be made by way of conclusion to this chapter. The distinction made above between educational theorising and philosophy of education, though useful as a heuristic strategy, is by no means so clear-cut as the account given might seem to suggest. The borderline between these two activities is not always well-defined and it is sometimes a matter of emphasis whether a writer may be said to be offering a theory or engaging in philosophy. Philosophers need not offer educational theories of their own, but they may do so, either explicitly, as Plato does, or implicitly, by registering approval or disapproval of an existing theory. A philosopher, for example, who tries to justify on rational grounds the adoption of a certain kind of curriculum is offering an educational theory. Another philosopher who wishes to criticise or reject the theory would by implication be giving support to a rival theory in its stead. The line where philosophical criticism of one theory passes over to the affirmation of another is a very fine one. Notwithstanding this blurring of the edges, however, it will still be helpful to think of theory as a body of overt recommendations for practice and philosophy as being the critical examination of such theories.

The second point is that while this book is *about* philosophy of education it will not confine itself to a description of what philosophers of education are trying to do. The best way of introducing philosophy is to do some philosophy and so from time to time in the following chapters some elementary philosophising will be tried out. A beginning has already been made. The distinction between theories which are primarily descriptive in function and those which are primarily prescriptive, involving a substantial commitment to some end thought desirable, is part of the analysis of what constitutes a theory, an analysis of the concept. Moreover, the point that, contrary to some popular belief, theory is logically prior to practice is itself a conclusion of philosophical interest, arising as it does out of an analysis of what counts as a practice.

### Suggestions for further reading

The 'revolution in philosophy' referred to in this chapter was a mainly technical matter and there are very few elementary works dealing with it. Perhaps the best introduction is J. Hospers, *An Introduction to Philosophical Analysis* (Routledge & Kegan Paul, 1967). This may be followed up by J.O. Urmson, *Philosophical Analysis* (Oxford University Press, 1956). Application of the new philosophical approach to the problems of education may be found in J. Archambault (ed.), *Philosophical Analysis and Education* (Routledge & Kegan Paul, 1965).

An elementary introduction to the nature of educational theory is given in T.W. Moore, *Educational Theory: An Introduction*. A more technical treatment of this topic may be found in papers by P.H. Hirst and D. J. O'Connor in *Proceedings of the Philosophy of Education Society of Great Britain*, vol. 6 (Basil Blackwell, 1972).

The scope of philosophy of education is dealt with in articles by P.H. Hirst and R.S. Peters in *The Study of Education* (ed. J. Tibble, Routledge & Kegan Paul, 1966), and in P.H. Hirst and R.S. Peters, *The Logic of Education.*

# General theory of education     2

## 1 Introduction

In chapter 1 it was maintained that philosophy of education consists largely of a critical comment on educational theory and that educational theory itself consists of a number of theories of varying scopes and complexities, ranging from simple theories about teaching to large-scale theories allied to, or associated with, some social, political or religious position. Much of the remainder of this book will be an attempt to show how general theories of education throw up topics of philosophical interest and how a philosopher of education might react to the pronouncements made in such theories. It will be useful here to indicate what would count as a topic of philosophical interest and what form a philosopher's reaction would be likely to take. By a 'topic of philosophical interest' is meant one which gives rise to questions of a conceptual nature, about the relationship between one concept and another, the relationship between 'education' and 'teaching', for example, or between 'authority' and 'power'; or one which reveals certain assumptions presupposed in an argument, assumptions which, being the basis of the argument, need to be established before the argument can be evaluated, assumptions about human nature, for example, or the nature of knowledge. Concepts, assumptions, and the arguments based on them are possible sources of philosophic interest, and the philosopher's reaction when confronted with them would be to look at the analysis of the concepts, to bring out as clearly as possible what was being said when they were used, to draw out and examine the assumptions and presuppositions involved in the argument, and then to evaluate the argument itself as being worthy of acceptance or not.

The nature of a general theory of education has already been indicated. A general theory differs from a limited theory in that it sets out to give a comprehensive programme for producing a certain type of person, an educated man, whereas a limited theory is concerned with particular educational issues, such as how this subject should be taught, or how children of this age and this ability should be dealt with. Plato, in *The Republic*, offers a number of limited theories of education, how to give children a sense of the orderliness and regularity of nature, how to deal with poets and poetry in education, how to make sure that the future soldiers are healthy and strong, and so on, but he does so within a general theory which aims at producing a certain type of individual, one capable of ruling the state. Rousseau's *Emile* contains many useful limited theories about sense training, physical training, training in self-reliance and in social awareness, but here too he offers these theories within the scope of a general theory designed to give what he calls an education 'according to nature' and to produce a 'natural man'. A general theory of education will thus contain within itself a number of particular and limited theories as part of its overall recommendations for practice. What characterises all such theories, however, limited or general, is a logical structure. Any practical theory will involve a set of assumptions or presuppositions which together form the basis of an argument. A general theory of education will involve presuppositions of a general kind. One of them will be a commitment to value, to some supposedly worthwhile end to be achieved; in this case some general notion of an educated man. There will also be assumptions about the raw material to be worked on, the nature of pupils, or more generally the nature of man; and assumptions about the nature of knowledge and skill and about the effectiveness of various pedagogical methods. These various assumptions will constitute the premisses of an argument whose conclusion will be a set of practical recommendations about what should be done in education.[12] Here, then, we have subject matter for the philosopher to work on: concepts like those of 'education' and the 'educated man', assumptions about ends to be achieved, about what is to count as an educated man, assumptions about the nature of knowledge and of methods, and an argument which is offered to support practical recommendations. These are the main centres of philosophical interest in this field.

This chapter will concentrate on an examination of two of these centres of interest: the assumptions made about education and its end, its aims and purposes; and the assumptions made about the nature of man.


## 2 Educational aims

The most important assumption made in a general theory of education is the assumption about the end to be achieved, the aim. This is a commitment to value and a logical prerequisite of there being a theory at all. All practical theories, limited or general, must begin with some notion of a desirable end to be attained. Formally a general theory of education can be said to have one aim only: to produce a certain type of person, an educated man. The interesting question is how to give substantial content to this formal aim. There are two ways in which this might be done. The first is to develop an analysis of the concept of education, to work out in detail the criteria which govern the actual use of this term. The criteria will be those which enable us to mark off the educated man from one who is not. The task of working out these criteria falls to the analytical philosopher of education. At the outset of this enterprise we meet with a complication. The term 'education' can be used in more than one way. In one of its uses it functions in a more or less descriptive way. A person's education may be understood as the sum total of his experiences. This is a perfectly acceptable use of the word, so that it would not be inappropriate to say of a man that his education came to him as a street urchin, or in a mining camp, or in the army. A more restricted use would be to use it to describe what happens to an individual in specifically educational institutions like schools or colleges. In this case to talk of a man's education is to talk of his passing through a system. 'He was educated at such-and-such a school' signifies that he went to the school in question. A more restricted sense still is one which imports into the notion of education some reference to value. Education, on this interpretation, is a normative or value term, and implies that what happens to the individual improves him in some way. The purely descriptive sense of the term carried no such implication; to comply in this case it is enough to have attended the school for a certain period. According to the normative use, an educated man is an improved man, and as such a desirable end-product, someone who ought to be produced. It is this normative sense of education which provides the logical starting-point of a general theory, the commitment to produce something of value, a desirable type of individual. Such a person would have specific characteristics, such as the possession of certain sorts of knowledge and skill, and the having of certain attitudes themselves regarded as worth having. The educated man would be one whose intellectual abilities had been developed, who was sensitive to matters of moral and aesthetic concern, who could appreciate the nature and force of mathematical and scientific thinking, who could view the world along historical and geographical perspectives and who, moreover, had a regard for the importance of truth, accuracy, and elegance in thinking. A further requirement is that the educated man is one whose knowledge and understanding is all of a piece, integrated, and not merely a mass of acquired information, piecemeal and unrelated. Taken all together these various criteria allow us to give content to the merely formal notion of the educated man by specifying what conditions have to be satisfied before the term has application.[16] The second way in which the aim may be given substance is to place it in some particular social, political or religious context. The formal aim simply demands an educated man, but this notion will vary in content according to the time, place and culture in which the aim is to be realised. For Plato the educated man was one trained in mathematical and philosophical disciplines, cognizant of true reality in his grasp of the Forms and both able and willing to act as guardian and ruler of the state.[19] For Herbert Spencer, living in an age and society very different from Plato's, the educated man was one who had acquired knowledge and intellectual development sufficient to enable him to support himself in an industrial and commercial society, to raise and support a family, to play the part of a citizen in such a society and to use his leisure wisely.[25] The kind of knowledge and skill which would have satisfied Plato's requirement would not have been much to the point in Spencer's England. James Mill, Thomas Arnold, Cardinal Newman and John Dewey each formulated a different notion of what would count as an educated man. Present-day shapers of societies, like the rulers of Cuba, emergent Africa, and China will no doubt have very different notions from those of nineteenth century Europe. Each will see the educated man in terms of what social demands will be made on such a man. It is perhaps worth mentioning here that the fact that the substance of the aim is bound to be culture-relative is a good reason why no general theory can provide recommendations applicable to all educational situations and why no such general theory will command universal acceptance. What is important, however, is the fact that common to all such theories is the assumption that the educated man is someone worth producing. This assumption establishes the educational aim, the logical point of departure for a general theory of education.

## 3 Aims and purposes in education

In talking about the aim, or aims, of education, a philosophical point has been made, namely, that an aim is a logical prerequisite of a practical theory. Unless some end is regarded as valuable no practical theory is possible. A practical theory consists simply of an argument providing recommendations for achieving some end thought desirable. Practice, it was maintained in chapter 1, is always theory-loaded. Another philosophical point which may be discussed here is that a distinction may be made between an 'aim' and a 'purpose'. This distinction may best be brought out by drawing attention to two different questions which may be put to someone who is engaged in a practical task. The questions are: what are you doing? and: what are you doing it for? To take the second of these questions first, to ask: What are you doing it for? is to presuppose some end outside the activity itself, which the activity is designed and intended to bring about. To the question: what are you learning French for? the answer might be: so that I can enjoy a holiday in France. The question: what are you digging that piece of ground for? could be answered by: so that I can grow potatoes in it. In both these examples the questions could have been put in terms of asking the *purpose* of the activity. In each case the answer is given in instrumental terms, one thing being done in order to achieve another, the end-product lying outside the activity itself. 'Purposes' point to ends external to an activity. A rather different approach is indicated in the first question: What are you doing? Here someone is being asked to specify what his action is, to state its content. The answers might in this case

27

be: I am trying to master the French language, or: I am digging over this piece of ground thoroughly. Here the explanation does not refer to any external end, it merely makes clear what is being done. In these cases it would be appropriate to ask the agent not about his purpose but about his *aim*. The question is: what exactly are you about? and the reply sets out his aim, what precisely he is about. The question about purpose is another question altogether. This point may be summed up by saying that whereas to talk of purposes is always to refer to some external end to which the activity is directed, to talk of aims is not to refer to external ends but to the activity itself, to its internal end. [16 chapter 1]

The distinction between aims and purposes is relevant to talk about education. A teacher may be asked to state his aim in a particular lesson, that is, to make clear what he is doing or trying to do. He may also be asked what is really a separate question, namely, why he is doing it, what he is doing it for, what his purpose is in trying to get his pupils to write poetry or to solve quadratic equations. So, too, it is possible to ask of education itself, what its aims are and what its purpose may be. The teacher's aims and purposes may be subsumed under the general headings of educational aims and purposes. Now, the aim of education, as has already been suggested, is to produce an educated man, one who meets the various criteria of intellectual, moral and aesthetic development. Education can, of course, be said to have subordinate aims, as, for example, the development of literary awareness, or the giving of an appreciation of scientific or mathematical modes of thinking, but taken all together these various subordinate aims coalesce in the overall end of making a certain kind of person. No reference is made here, however, to any good *outside* education. It is quite another question to ask: what is education for? What is the purpose of it? Answers to this question are different from those given in response to questions about aims. The purpose of education, it might be said, is to increase the number of literate, knowledgeable citizens, or to produce sufficient numbers of doctors, lawyers, civil servants, engineers and the like. Here the reference is to valuable ends which lie outside the actual practice of education, social, political or economic ends. This is an important conceptual point. To ask the aim of education is to conceive of education as an end in itself, something intrinsically good, involving the development of a person. To ask its purpose or purposes is to think of it as a device designed to bring about external goods, skilled workers, executives, professionals. It is because of this distinction that it is often said that the aims of education are internal and that it is inappropriate to ask for an aim which lies outside education itself. Education is a good as such; this is a conceptual truth derived from the normative meaning of 'education'. In fact the aim of any activity is internal to it, since to ask about an aim is to ask to be told what the activity is; but not all activities are, or need be, good in themselves; education is so. An unfortunate result of a recognition that education is intrinsically valuable is the conclusion that to go further and ask the purpose of education is a trifle ill-bred. Education, it may be thought, being an end in itself should not be regarded in terms of purpose. There is, however, no warrant for this kind of exclusiveness. There is a sense in which education is a good *per se,*

29

and its own reward. But it makes good sense to ask: why do we want well-developed, sensitive, intellectually equipped, useful people? and to receive an answer in terms of social and political well-being. The educated man needs also to be a good citizen, a good worker, a good colleague, and being educated may be, indeed should be, a great help in achieving these worthwhile external ends. Education has important purposes as well as important aims.

## 4 Assumptions about human nature

A general theory of education begins, logically, with an assumption about an end, the notion of an educated man. To realise this end it recommends certain pedagogical procedures for practice. But between the aim and the procedures there must be certain assumptions made about the raw material, the person to be educated. It has to be assumed that human nature is to some extent malleable, that what happens to the pupil by way of experience has some lasting effect on his subsequent behaviour. There would be no point in trying to teach children if whatever was done could make no difference to them. This assumption is, like the assumption about aims, a logical prerequisite of education taking place at all, and it is a matter of philosophical interest that such an assumption is one that not merely may be made but *must* be made. Apart from this logical assumption there are others which, as a matter of fact, may be made about human nature. Here we run into another area of philosophical concern. The non-logical, contingent assumptions about pupils which would be of most use to educational theorists would be those based on the results of empirical enquiry and evidence. It is the failure to adopt assumptions based on such evidence which vitiates a good deal of what was offered by the historical general theorists. In the past assumptions of a substantial nature about children were often derived, supposedly, from metaphysical or religious views of the nature of man, and were seldom based on any systematic examination of actual men or children. It was sometimes assumed, for example, that man's nature was essentially sinful and that this fact of original sin had to be provided against when dealing with children. The Calvinist notion of 'driving out the old Adam' was considered to have significant practical implications for schoolmasters. Rousseau, by contrast, rejected entirely the belief in man's original sinfulness and held that children, although not born morally good, were nonetheless essentially good in that they were wholly lacking in original corruption.[21] An objection to both these assumptions is that no experience of actual children would serve to falsify them. A child of angelic disposition would not falsify the Calvinistic assumption, since it would be assumed that his wickedness had been driven out, not that he was originally free of it. A thoroughly vicious child would not falsify Rousseau's assumption since Rousseau was wont to explain vice as the result of corruption by society. Neither Calvin nor Rousseau ever tried to establish these assumptions by finding out what children in general are like. The assumptions they made were made *a priori*, in advance of any empirical evidence. Another celebrated assumption about children was Locke's contention that they are born *tabula rasa*, cognitively empty. This could be true in fact, although modern linguistic theorists like

Chomsky to some extent question it. Locke, however, tended to argue its truth without making any serious empirical enquiries to establish it. Much the same may be said of Froebel's unargued view that each child exemplifies a divine pattern of development which needs to be realised in his life, and which it is the purpose of education to realise. [5]

A general criticism of assumptions like these is that they are of the wrong kind for a theory of education. They are *a priori* assumptions, adopted ahead of experience, and often of the kind that experience can do nothing to confirm or refute. What is needed in an educational theory is an accurate factual picture of human nature, especially of child nature, and this can come only from studies which set out deliberately to discover what children are like. Here we have a further philosophical point of some importance. It is this: if we want to discover some truth about the world, about what exists in it or what is likely to happen in it, we have to begin by examining the world, by observation and experiment. No help is given by making assumptions prior to experience about what is the case or what is likely to happen. So Froebel's assumption about child nature is virtually useless as an aid to educational practice. To say that a child's nature will develop according to a predetermined divine pattern, or should be helped to do so, is to say no more than that it will develop as it will. Whatever the outcome it will be compatible with this assumption. Those made by Calvin and by Rousseau do not help very much either. What educational practitioners need to know about children: how they develop, how they may be motivated and managed, what may be expected of them at different stages in their development, will come from scientific studies of children themselves. Piaget, Freud, Kohlberg and other child-study specialists have more to offer in this respect than the great names in traditional educational theory.

## 5 Two approaches to general theory of education

We may now broaden the approach to educational theory by outlining two major assumptions which have been made about human nature, assumptions which differ radically in their emphasis and which, when adopted, have given radically different directions to educational practice. The assumptions reflect what may be called mechanistic and organic accounts of phenomena.

Amongst the various entities which exist in the world some are quite obviously contrivances of one kind or another. Others are obviously organisms, or living creatures. A clock is an example of the first kind, a vegetable an example of the second. A crucial difference between them is that contrivances are usually although not invariably man-made, whereas organic entities are not man-made but are 'natural' in the way that no human contrivance can be. This distinction may be utilised, by analogy, to gain insights into the workings and behaviour of entities and organisations which are not really like clocks or vegetables, for example, society, or the state, or a man. Thomas Hobbes, in writing *Leviathan*, likened a man to a wonderfully contrived machine, composed of springs, wheels and levers.[8] This is perhaps the way in which an anatomist might regard a human being, as a kind of machine, involving moving parts. Of course a man is more than a machine, as a clock is not, but it may be useful or convenient sometimes to view men in this way, to give a simplified model of what is in reality very complex. Hobbes adopted this model because he wanted to pursue a particular line of political argument, to depict human society itself as a contrivance made up of individuals who themselves could be regarded in this way. The organic approach, of, for instance, Froebel, by contrast, takes as its model the view of an entity as a living, growing, developing creature, a 'natural' whole.[5] Here the various elements which constitute it are not simply integrated into a system of checks and balances, cogs and levers, as in the case of a machine, but form a whole which functions as an entity which is more important than the sum of its parts. The parts are regarded as living tissues which taken together constitute the whole. The whole is logically prior to its parts, in the sense that the parts exist only as parts of a whole. Thus a man is more than an assemblage of bones and muscles, nerves and sinews, and, as Hegel and his followers would have it, a society is something more than the totality of individuals who compose it. A machine too is composed of subordinate parts, but it is nothing more than the organised sum of its parts, its 'wholeness' is simply an aggregate of parts. An organism is a whole which transcends its parts. Moreover, unlike a machine an organism is capable of growth and development; it has an internal dynamic principle which helps to determine its history.

Now, as suggested above, it is possible, and it may sometimes be useful, to make assumptions about human nature based upon this mechanistic – organic distinction.

There is a sense in which a man is like a machine, a system of inputs and outputs, one which can work effectively or ineffectively. This much could be established by empirical enquiry and any assumption of this kind would be scientifically respectable. It would not of course be the whole story. To regard a man simply as a machine would be to ignore what is essentially human in him. Nonetheless it may sometimes be the case that man is best understood in mechanistic terms. The organic model offers an alternative account which seems, prima facie at any rate, to be a more plausible basis for an adequate view of man, emphasising as it does his capacity for growth and development. This model has advantages and disadvantages, perhaps the most telling disadvantage being its tendency to lead towards vagueness and unquantifiable assertions about feelings, aspirations and the like. In fact, though both models have their uses it is as well not to press either analogy too far. Neither of them, alone, gives an adequate picture; both may be useful as models, simplified versions of reality. The point of introducing them here is to suggest that they may each feature as a fundamental assumption about human nature and underpin a general theory of education. Moreover they are both assumptions for which there is some empirical justification.

Translated into an educational context these two approaches would take different forms. An educational theory framed on mechanistic assumptions would hold that man is a kind of machine. As with any machine, effective working would be revealed by performance, which in a man would be his external behaviour. Education would be one of the means of making his external

35

responses as effective as possible. A pupil would be seen as a device whose workings could be deliberately regulated from without. He would not 'grow' or 'develop' according to some internal dynamic: rather his behaviour would be modified or 'shaped' to approach some desirable end, like living harmoniously and happily in a society composed of individuals like himself. Teaching would be a matter of organising desirable inputs — knowledge, skills and attitudes. The educated man would be one whose behavioural outputs met the criteria of worthwhileness adopted by his society. A general theory of education based on an organic view of man would tend to emphasise just those aspects of the pupil which a mechanistic view would ignore: the internal principles of development and growth. The organic assumption is that the pupil is essentially a 'growing' creature and this would mean that education would be, not a modification or shaping from without, but an attempt to encourage individual development from within, involving organic growth rather than a mechanical adaptation to environmental pressures. [21] [5]

These two approaches, stated briefly and summarily here, spring from radically different assumptions or presuppositions about the nature of man. They have had considerable and significant influence on educational theory and practice. Historically, the mechanistic approach has been adopted by the French philosopher Helvetius, James Mill [11] and, more recently, by B.F. Skinner.[26] Helvetius adopted the model in such an uncompromising way as to suggest that this deliberate manipulation of the pupil's environment would enable the educator to make virtually anything he wished out of the pupil. *Education peut tout* was a slogan which derived from this approach. The organic view is exemplified by Rousseau and his many disciples and imitators, Froebel for example, and Dewey. Faced with educational theories of these kinds, the task of the philosopher of education is to draw out and make explicit such assumptions and to enter certain caveats against them. This has already been done to some extent above. It has been suggested that neither of them should be regarded as anything more than an analogous description, and neither of these models should be taken too literally. They are not wholly divorced from empirical evidence, but each tends to give a one-sided view of the whole. Nonetheless, as analogies they have their uses. They provide useful ways of looking at the practice of education, and each assumption does service in drawing attention to aspects of human nature which the other might play down or ignore. The historical theorists tended to adopt one or the other as complete accounts of human nature and to this extent these historical theories are themselves one-sided. A better way of utilising the analogies is to recognise that each offers a different perspective in education, and that neither of them should be supposed to give a complete or comprehensive view.


## 6 Conclusion

The first chapter in this book set out the nature and scope of philosophy of education and tried to show what philosophers of education are trying to do. The present chapter indicates some of the philosophical moves that might be made. It takes as its starting-point

37

the idea of a general theory of education. Central to the logical structure of a general theory of education are certain assumptions without which such a theory could not operate at all. Two of these basic assumptions are then examined. The first was the assumption that prior to any recommendations for educational practice there must be some desirable end to be achieved, this desirable end being formally expressed as an educated man. The second assumption, or set of assumptions, concerned the nature of man, the raw material of education. In the course of the chapter some elementary points of philosophical significance were introduced: the distinction between educational aims and educational purposes, a brief analysis of the concept of education, and the point that answers to questions about empirical matters, for example questions about the nature of children, must be derived from empirical enquiry and not assumed ahead of empirical evidence. Finally, an attempt was made to bring out the general assumptions about human nature which underlie some historically important theories of education, assumptions which reflect the distinction between mechanistic and organic views of man.

## Suggestions for further reading

P.H. Hirst and R.S. Peters, *The Logic of Education*, chapter 2, contains a discussion of the aims of education. A symposium on this topic, *Aims of Education — A Conceptual Inquiry* by R.S. Peters, J. Woods and W.H. Dray appears in *The Philosophy of Education* (ed. R.S. Peters, Oxford University Press, 1975).

The various assumptions about human nature made

by past educational theorists have to be studied in the original texts, references to which are given in the bibliography. A discussion of the assumptions made by some of the more important theorists is given in T.W. Moore, *Educational Theory: An Introduction*, chapters 3 and 4.

# 3   Knowledge and the curriculum

## 1 Introduction

The analysis of the concept of education attempted in the previous chapter suggested that the educated man would be one who had acquired some worthwhile knowledge, understanding and skills. What knowledge, what sorts of understanding and what skills will come under this heading will depend on the kind of society which does the educating, but any society sophisticated enough to have a concept of education must regard some knowledge and some skills as worth passing on to the next generation. Indeed, a society's future will depend upon this cultural transmission. This corpus of knowledge and skill will constitute a curriculum, and a general theory of education must involve some assumptions about the curriculum, about what must be taught. These assumptions will be those about the nature of knowledge and this chapter sets out to examine what is involved in this concept. A preliminary distinction needs to be made, however, between the curriculum and the rules for educational practice, between *what* is taught and *how* it is taught. In what follows the curriculum will be understood as the *content* of education, *what* is taught. Educational practice and methods come under the heading of pedagogy which will be dealt with in the next chapter.

The curriculum, then, is a matter of knowledge and skills to be passed on to pupils. Traditionally, the curriculum breaks down into different subject areas or disciplines, mathematics, science, history and so on, but generally the curriculum may be considered simply as a body of knowledge which it is thought ought to be transmitted to others. So far as a general theory of education goes, the curriculum is one of the means by which the overall aim is translated into achievement: educated men and women are formed by being introduced to and initiated into various kinds of knowledge and skill. The philosopher of education is interested in two aspects of this: firstly, in an analysis of the concept of knowledge and its relation with other concepts, like belief and truth, and secondly, in the question of what knowledge and skills should be taught, what knowledge is worth having. The educational theorist recommends, for example, that educating a man involves teaching him mathematics, science, history and the other traditional disciplines. The philosopher asks: why these subjects? why this knowledge and these skills? In other words the philosopher has to do with analysis and justification. His questions are: what is knowledge? and: what knowledge is of most worth?

## 2 What is knowledge?

This question is really two questions in one, and each raises issues of considerable complexity. The two questions are: what is knowledge in general, what exactly is it that can be known? and: what does it mean to say of anyone that he knows something? The answer to either of these questions would require a book in

41

itself, and what follows in this chapter can be no more than a brief and elementary account of the main issues involved.

## Knowledge in general

The question we try to answer here is: what is knowledge about? what are we talking about when we talk about knowledge as such? One answer to this question was given by Plato [19] who made a clear distinction between knowledge and belief and restricted knowledge to the apprehension of certain non-sensible objects which he called 'Forms' or 'Ideas'. These objects stand outside the world of everyday things, outside space and time, and can be known only by a kind of intuitive grasp which comes, Plato thought, from a special kind of quasi-mathematical training. The objects of the everyday world, trees, rocks, clouds, men and the like cannot, strictly, be known about, since for Plato knowledge involved a special kind of certainty. Whatever is known, he thought, must be known indubitably, and it seemed plain to him that we could have no certainty about the everchanging world of everyday things. About this world, a world of phenomena or appearances, we could have only opinion or beliefs. Knowledge was a matter of grasping necessary truths about a non-phenomenal world, necessary in the sense that it was impossible to be mistaken about them. A development of this view led, in the seventeenth century, to what is called the rationalist tradition, associated with philosophers like Descartes, Spinoza and Leibnitz, in which knowledge is regarded as analogous to the grasping of mathematical truths. This view may be characterised by saying that it holds mathematics to be the paradigm example of knowledge. It is easy to see why mathematics should be chosen as a paradigm. For mathematical truths are universal: they are truths always, everywhere. Moreover, they are necessary truths. Three times three must be nine: the internal angles of a triangle must add up to 180 degrees. To deny these propositions would not merely be an error: it would be a self-contradiction. Mathematical reasoning is demonstrative, or deductive. It has the comforting characteristic that if its initial premises are accepted and the correct procedure followed, the conclusion follows of necessity. The rationalist philosophers were attracted by this model of knowledge and they tried to use it to establish certain and necessary truths about the actual world, truths which they thought could be derived from self-evident principles and grasped as we grasp the truths of mathematics and logic.

An alternative view takes science as a paradigm. Here knowledge is not a matter of deduction from self-evident principles, but comes as the result of observation and experiment in the empirical world. The order and regularity with which our experiences occur enables us to make large-scale generalisations about the contents and events of the world, which we can use to explain and predict the course of future experience. This is the empiricist model of knowledge, associated with philosophers like Hume and James Mill, which sees substantial knowledge not as a body of necessary truths but as contingent conclusions, depending on the way the empirical world happens in fact to be. It happens to be the case that fire burns, that sugar tastes sweet, that gases expand when heated; it might have been otherwise. This conclusion may be put in this way: the contrary of any empirical truth is always possible, whereas the contrary of a mathematical truth is logically impossible and so absurd. Uncompromising empiricist philosophers like the Logical Positivists of the 1930s held that all substantial, informative knowledge was of this contingent kind. Mathematical knowledge, they maintained, was not substantial or informative of the actual world. Such knowledge was purely formal, a matter of definitions and derivations from them, the conclusions of which were necessarily true simply because of the way in which the various terms were defined.

Both the rationalist and the empiricist accounts of knowledge seem to be one-sided and so not wholly adequate. The defect of the rationalist adherence to the mathematical paradigm is that necessary truths, though certain, give no substantial information. It is forever true that the internal angles of a triangle add up to 180 degrees but this tells us nothing about the actual existence of triangles. The proposition would be true even if no triangles existed. Truths of this kind are formal, necessary, but empty, and attempts by the rationalists to arrive at necessary truths about the empirical world could not be successful. On the other hand, empirical generalisations are true only in so far as there is evidence to support them, and there is always the possibility that fresh evidence may show them to be false. Thus empirical propositions purport to give substantial information about the world but they are never logically certain or necessarily true; propositions in mathematics and logic when true are necessarily true but give no substantial information about the world. This dilemma tends to produce considerable intellectual discomfort, since if taken strictly it would preclude us from ever claiming to have knowledge of the world we live in, knowledge, that is, which carries with it the requirement of strict certainty. This issue is complicated by the fact that we seem to have an inescapable conviction that there is a kind of necessity inherent in the world, that what happens in it has something more than a mere contingency. Two attempts were made in the eighteenth century to account for this conviction of necessity. David Hume, a Scottish empiricist, recognised that, apart from logic and mathematics, there were no necessarily true propositions, but he held that we nonetheless project a kind of necessity into our account of the world. Our regular and uniform experiences lead us to expect events to occur as they do, although we have no other warrant for this expectation than our previous experience. [9] It is our previous experience which prompts us to conclude that much of what does happen *must* happen. We expect that causes will have the effects they do have, and that objects will behave as they normally do, and we come to conclude that there is a necessity in what happens. This conviction of necessity was, for Hume, a matter of psychology. Kant, however, argued that in experiencing the world as we do we necessarily do so under certain conditions. We can only experience the world as we do on the assumption that the world is a causal system operating in space and time. Kant holds that we can only experience the world under certain forms and categories of the mind, which structure our experience and give it a framework of necessity.[10] The difference between Hume's version and Kant's is that whilst Hume sees this structuring of our experience as a psychological necessity for us, Kant holds it to be a logical prerequisite of our knowing or even experiencing at all.

We may conclude this section by pointing out that the accounts given by Hume and Kant do no more than try to explain how it is that we have the conviction that there is a kind of inevitability about much that happens in our experience. It does not mean that all that we know is necessarily true. Some of what we know *is* necessarily true, the truths of mathematics for example. But we do not have to adopt an extreme rationalist view and exclude from knowledge all that is not necessarily true, the truths of science for instance. Plato's view of knowledge as being necessary and incorrigible, absolutely immune from error, is far too stringent and restrictive. We can properly claim to *know* truths which do not amount to necessary truths. Indeed, most of our knowledge is of this kind.

### 'Knowing'

So far we have been dealing with knowledge in general terms. We have asked: what is knowledge *of* or *about*? The answers, once again stated generally, have been: necessary truths, as in mathematics, or empirical truths, as in the sciences. Of course there are other possible areas of knowledge, everyday sorts of knowledge like knowing that the garden gate is painted green, moral knowledge, aesthetic knowledge, perhaps religious knowledge, about all of which there has been considerable discussion and dispute amongst philosophers. In this section we will ask, not: what is knowledge about? but: what has to be the case before anyone can properly be said to know anything? Another way of putting this would be: what are the conditions of knowledge? or: what analysis can be given of the concept of knowledge? Or again: what justification is required to substantiate a claim that something is known? Such questions about analysis and justification are, of course, typically philosophers' questions.

The analysis of the concept of knowledge and the justification of a claim to know are very closely bound up together and there will be some difficulty in separating them. We may begin with the analysis. The word 'know' is a verb, so it might be supposed that to know something is to perform some 'inner' mental action, that knowing is a performance of some kind. This, however, will not do. I can know that something is the case without making any specific performance. I know who designed St Paul's Cathedral even when I'm not thinking about Sir Christopher Wren, when I'm asleep or when I'm thinking about something quite different. Nor would it be appropriate for me to say that I'm busy knowing something, as I could properly say that I'm busy writing or reading. 'Knowing' isn't the name of an activity, as 'running' or 'reading' or 'writing' is. It is better to think of it as what Ryle [22] calls an 'achievement' word. To know that p is the case is to claim to have had a success. In an educational context we would use the term with others like 'learning', 'enquiring' or 'studying'. If we apply ourselves to mastering some topic, we will, if successful, come to know something. Some cognitive position will have been successfully occupied. To know that p is the case is to be in a certain position in respect to p: roughly, it is to be in a position to guarantee the truth of the proposition concerned. Actually to be in this privileged position is a justification of the claim to know.

The important question now is: what conditions have to be satisfied before anyone can properly be said to be in this privileged position? The first requirement is that the proposition p must be true. Not *necessarily* true in the sense that to deny it would amount to a self-contradiction, but true as a matter of fact. Unless p really is so, no one can justifiably claim to know that it is so. It is, of course, possible to make the claim, but the claim made would not stand up to scrutiny. Medieval man may have claimed to know that the earth was flat, but such a claim would be defeated by the facts. No one could ever have known that the earth was flat, simply because it isn't and never was flat. The next requirement is that the person making the claim must be sure that p is so. It would be odd, logically odd, to say: 'I know that p is so but I'm not really sure about it.' It would be logically odd because it would run counter to the generally accepted usage of the term 'know'. The third condition is that the  person making the claim must be able to cite evidence and evidence of the right kind to support his claim. If evidence were not forthcoming then we would think it more appropriate to say that he believed rather than knew, as we would do in the case of a person who declared that he was not sure. These three conditions, that p must be true, that the claimant must be sure, and, moreover, have evidence to support his claim, constitute an analysis of the concept of knowing by providing criteria for its correct application.[1] When, and to the extent that, these conditions are met we would be prepared to concede that the claimant was in the privileged position of being able to endorse or guarantee the truth of the proposition. It is important to note that what is being referred to here is a *claim*, and that this claim is defeasible. It would be weakened, for instance, if it turned out that the claimant wasn't sure, or if he couldn't produce evidence. It would be completely defeated if it were established that p was false. Lack of space here forbids a discussion of cases where a weaker version of knowing would be acceptable, as for example where a child knows but is temporarily flustered in an examination and so is unsure about what he would otherwise be confident about, or where someone consistently gets the right answer although he can't bring evidence to support his claim. What has been outlined here is the standard, paradigm sense of the term, giving those criteria which must be satisfied if, in normal conditions, the claim to know is to be admitted.

Two points of philosophical interest arise out of this analysis. The first is that although 'knowing' doesn't itself name an activity or performance, we should need to apply behavioural criteria to discover whether or not someone was in the special position that knowing implies. If we want to find out whether a child knows his seven-times table or the date of the Spanish Armada, we have to get him to *do* something, to recite the table or write down the date. If he consistently gives a correct performance we would say that he knows. But his giving a correct performance when required isn't what is *meant* by his knowing; it is simply good evidence that he knows. His knowing consists in his being able to give the correct answer. The second point is that the concept of knowledge is closely bound up with the concept of truth. A justified claim to know entails the truth of the proposition known. We could not have the concept of knowledge unless we also had the concept of truth. The philosopher of education will therefore be concerned with this other concept and ask: what is being said when it is asserted that a given proposition is true? The literature on this topic is immense and no attempt to deal with it in detail is possible in an elementary book of this kind. An account which, despite shortcomings, is probably as satisfactory as any, is that the qualification 'is true' is best seen as an evaluation. To say 'p is true' is to rate p high up on a scale of preference, tantamount to saying, 'Accept p!', or 'Act on the assumption of p!' This grading or recommendation of p will depend on some rationale, for example, that there is empirical evidence to support the high rating. It would be good evidence for the truth of 'The cat is on the mat' if there actually was a cat on the mat. This would warrant the recommendation that the assertion be adopted. Similarly, if it could be shown that a proposition coheres with others in a formal system like arithmetic or geometry, this too would be sufficient to support the recommendation that it be adopted, rated high, characterised as 'true'. Again, a reason for saying that 'p is true' would be that if we act on this assumption we get good results in practice. In this way what are usually called the classical theories of truth, correspondence with the facts, coherence within a system, or pragmatic efficiency, can be used to indicate what kind of support is needed to justify the valuation contained in the assertion that a given statement is true.


## 3 'Knowing that', 'knowing how' and 'believing'

In the section above the discussion has been almost

entirely in terms of knowing that something is the case, with what is called propositional or theoretical knowledge. There is of course a wide area of knowledge which consists in knowing *how* to do something, to solve problems, to speak French, to play the violin and so on. So obviously the analysis given above needs to be extended. Knowing how to play the violin doesn't depend crucially on my holding any propositions to be true. Basically, however, the situation here is similar to that given in the previous analysis. To know *how* to do something, to be adept or skilled in some respect, is to be in a certain privileged position, to be able to give an appropriate performance. There is an easy way of finding out whether anyone knows how to play the violin or to speak French. We ask him to exhibit his skill in some way. But here again, the giving of a correct or appropriate performance isn't what is *meant* by knowing how to do it. The 'knowing how' is the being in a position to do whatever is required. This superior position is analogous to the logically superior position of one who can justifiably claim to know that something is the case.

There is, moreover, a certain reciprocity between 'knowing that' and 'knowing how'. If I know that p is the case I also know *how* to answer certain questions about p; and if I know how to perform some operation I may well be in a position to make correct statements about what I am doing and how I am doing it. This may not always be the case, however. It often happens that someone may have a skill and yet be unable to say much about how he gets his results. It is not easy to make true statements about how one balances on a bicycle or how one is able to swim, even if one knows very well how to do either.

The distinction between 'knowing that' and 'knowing how' is not parallelled in the associated concept of believing. We may believe *that* something is the case, but we never believe 'how'. There are, nonetheless, certain parallelisms and some significant differences between knowing and believing. As is the case with knowing, believing is not an activity. We can't be interrupted in the middle of believing something, nor can we be too busy believing to do anything else. As with 'knowing', 'believing' indicates that a certain position has been reached; to believe is to take up a certain stance in respect of a proposition. It is to accept the proposition as true. To believe that p is the case is simply to accept the truth of p. This does not imply that in believing one is in a position to endorse or to guarantee the *truth* of p. We may believe p when p is not true. Moreover, belief does not require that we should have evidence for our stance, or even that we should feel sure about our position. Indeed we should be most likely to say that we believed in just those cases where we weren't altogether sure, or where evidence was in some degree lacking. There is, however, a parallelism with knowledge in that if we want to find out what a person believes we must inspect his behaviour. 'Knowing' and 'believing' both refer to positions reached. We discover when, or if, these positions have been reached by finding out what the claimant is disposed to say or do.

We may round off this section by referring briefly to a concept closely linked with knowing but which cannot be simply equated with it, the concept of understanding. The equation can't be made because there would seem to be instances where we may be said to know that something is the case but, nonetheless, not understand what is involved in it. A child might learn, mechanically, that the area of a circle can be expressed as $\pi r^2$ and so be said to know that this is true, and yet have no grasp of the implications of this truth. To understand what is involved in it would require an ability to put this information to some use, be able, for example, to calculate the radius of a circle given its area. Understanding entails knowledge, but it also involves our being able to use this knowledge. It is a special sort of knowing, 'knowing how to go on'. We understand when we are able to give good reasons for making the next appropriate move.

## 4 Knowledge and the curriculum

We have now to turn to the second line of enquiry, that of justification. The educational curriculum is primarily a matter of knowledge, knowing that and knowing how, together with some beliefs and attitudes, all of which it is thought desirable that children should be introduced to. The question is: what knowledge, what beliefs and what attitudes? Plainly, not everything which counts as knowledge and most certainly not everything that can be believed would be suitable for inclusion in an educational curriculum. Lack of time alone would require that a selection should be made from the vast amount of knowledge available. Moreover, the normative sense of education requires that what is taught should be worth learning, capable of improving the person who learns. So the question may be put as: what knowledge is of most worth? Different answers to this question will result in different conclusions about the curriculum. Now, it is perhaps important to note that few teachers are in real doubt as to what the curriculum should include. Most teachers would be surprised and puzzled if they went into a school which did not teach mathematics, some science, history, geography, some aesthetic subjects and some religious and moral content. These are areas of knowledge and belief generally accepted as worth teaching to children. The main question to be asked about the contents of the curriculum is not: what knowledge is to be included? but: what grounds are there for holding that the traditional curriculum should be as it is? We have a general conviction about what knowledge is of most worth. The problem is to make clear why we have this conviction. This is a problem about which the philosopher of education may have something useful to say, since it is a problem about justification.

Different answers to the question: why should we teach *these* subjects or *these* disciplines rather than any others? really amount to different theories of the curriculum. They are subordinate prescriptive theories which find their place within the framework of a general theory of education. They come under the heading of 'assumptions about knowledge'. The assumptions are to the effect that certain kinds of knowledge are necessary to realise the educational aim presupposed by the overall theory. In the remainder of this chapter some major theories of the curriculum will be outlined.

*The 'utilitarian' curriculum*

The word 'utilitarian' may be understood in two different although related ways. It may be equated roughly with 'useful', so that a utilitarian curriculum would be one justified on the grounds that the subjects included in it were useful to the learner. Mathematics may be justified because it is useful, to the workman, the householder, the engineer, the scientist. So too with science. One influential educationalist of the nineteenth century, Herbert Spencer, thought that scientific knowledge was at the bottom of all that one needed to know in order to be a competent worker, successful parent, responsible citizen and wise user of leisure. Apart from mathematics and science, other disciplines - history, geography, and the various arts and crafts - may be justified on the grounds that they too are useful in one way or another. This view of the curriculum is revealed in Rousseau's *Emile*, in which it is held that everything Emile learns should be justified in terms of 'what use is this to me?' [21]

Another, more restricted meaning of the term is, roughly, 'conducive to human happiness'. This was the view of those philosophers known as Utilitarians, who held that the point of human activity should be to promote the greatest amount of happiness for the largest possible number of people. One of the leading Utilitarians James Mill, declared that it was the business of education to make the human mind the source of happiness, both to the individual himself and to others. [11] So a strictly Utilitarian curriculum would be justified on the grounds that it conduced towards human happiness. Happiness, the Utilitarians thought, was largely a matter of the way in which the external world of things and the social world of neighbours and institutions made an impact on men's lives, and education was a way of preparing the pupil to live happily in these worlds. Science, for example, enables us to foresee the consequences of our actions and their effect on our own happiness and that of others by introducing us to a system of regularities, causes and effects. This kind of knowledge is, literally, power. So too history and the social sciences, politics and morals enable us to predict with some degree of accuracy the reactions of our fellows in our dealings with them. Religious knowledge, in so far as there is any such, enables us to look to our happiness here and hereafter. The traditional curriculum, the arts and sciehces, may be justified simply because the various disciplines included in it have been found to conduce to happiness, not only that of the learner himself, but also of all those with whom he comes into social contact.

It may be useful to refer briefly here to a position maintained in recent years by the sociologists of education who, following a Marxist line of thought, point out that an educational curriculum in fact reflects an interest. [28] The knowledge included is that which, by and large, is in the interest of those whose ideas are predominantly influential in society. The curriculum, in other words, reflects the interest of a social class. On this view the Utilitarian curriculum of the nineteenth century reflected the interests of the commercial and industrial middle class whose social position was then dominant, and such a curriculum is not necessarily appropriate to a different social situation, with different class interests. An extension and implication of this position is that there can be no 'absolute' knowledge since what counts as knowledge will always be socially determined and therefore relative. It is not possible to deal here with the interesting but complicated further implications of this position. What can be said here is that this 'relativist' theory of knowledge contains a truth obscured by a muddle. The truth is that what counts as *worthwhile* knowledge and skill will be socially determined. Different kinds of societies and societies at different stages of development will have different views on what knowledge is worthwhile. But it doesn't follow from this that, as is sometimes suggested, society makes its own knowledge, that knowledge is, by its nature, socially determined and relative The truths of applied mathematics and science, for example, do not depend on what men think or decide, although the value of these disciplines will to a large extent do so.

## A curriculum for rationality

The idea that a curriculum is justified to the extent to which it produces a 'rational mind' is as old as Plato. The curriculum outlined in *The Republic* was designed to produce the sort of man who would be able to apprehend the Forms of reality which lay behind the shifting appearances of the everyday world. Plato's curriculum involved certain initial empirical studies for the young child, to acquaint him with the order which exists in the phenomenal world, but the emphasis soon shifts to more formal studies for the young men destined to become the Guardians of the state. These formal studies involved mathematics – for Plato the paradigm of knowledge, and a sort of philosophy akin to mathematics, which would eventually yield true knowledge, a quasi-mathematical grasping or intuition of the Forms. Such knowledge would be true knowledge, a rational grasp of reality, as distinct from the opinions men may have, which are all they can have, of the world of appearances.

A modern theory of the curriculum which, despite many significant differences, has some points of similarity with the Platonic view, is that offered by P.H. Hirst. [6] Hirst's account is that, historically, men have adopted certain ways of looking at their world, certain 'forms of knowledge' as he calls them. They may perhaps be best understood, not as entities in the Platonic sense, but as different perspectives, giving different viewpoints concerning the world. Each form has its own characteristic conceptual structure and a characteristic way of coming to conclusions. Mathematics is one such form, with its own set of concepts, like 'number', 'square root', 'cosine', and its characteristic procedures, deductive argument and demonstration. Science is another form of knowledge, once again with its characteristic concepts, such as mass energy, protoplasm, and osmosis, and its own characteristic ways of arriving at conclusions: observation, experiment, inductive reasoning. Other forms are those of morals, aesthetics and religion, each of which has its own conceptual apparatus and its own particular way of arriving at conclusions and testing those conclusions for truth. This theory has not been fully worked out in detail and there are still unanswered questions concerning it. The tests for truth in morals, aesthetics and religion, for example, have not been clearly set out or even established so far as to meet general acceptance. The point about the theory, however, is that it offers a justification of the curriculum as a means of the making of a mind, a rational mind. Hirst's major recommendation is that, since each form is separate and distinct and no one form is a substitute for another, the curriculum should contain all the forms of knowledge if a rational mind is to be fashioned by it. For rationality is a matter of acting for good reasons, and good reasons ultimately depend on knowledge. So, unless the pupil is initiated into all the forms of knowledge there must be areas of human experience in which he will not be able to act for good reasons. A man who knows no science cannot act rationally within a scientific context. In so far as he acts effectively it will be by chance, or, more likely, as a result of being directed by someone who does have the required knowledge. Anyone who has not been initiated into the arts, music or literature will be unable to make rational decisions or choices in these fields, will not be able to act with rational autonomy. The same will be true of anyone whose learning is quite outside the area of religious belief or moral knowledge. That knowledge will be of most worth which prepares the pupil for rational living, by giving him the intellectual basis of rational action. The traditional curriculum is justified to the extent to which it provides such a preparation.

## A 'heritage' curriculum

Another theory of justification, not altogether different from the preceding one, might be put in this way: the point of education is to bring children into what exists as a public tradition of shared knowledge. This public tradition may be seen as a kind of heritage, an estate in which all members of the human race have an interest, a part or a place. Another word for the tradition or estate is 'culture', and culture comprises the intellectual, aesthetic, moral and material achievements of mankind in its long history. Mathematics and science are a part of this heritage; so too are music and painting and architecture. So too are morality and the religious point of view. History is a part of it, since history is about man's past; geography is a part of it, since geography is about man's place in the physical world. These different areas of knowledge and belief constitute a human outlook on reality. To be able to move about freely in these areas is to be a human being, as distinct from a human animal. A human being is one who is able to understand his situation in these terms. Children are not born with this understanding. They are born human, but they are born human animals rather than human beings. Education is the means by which the human animal is converted into a human being. Or, in other words, the means by which the child is brought into the systems of shared knowledge which constitute his cultural heritage or estate. [15] The curriculum is justified to the extent to which it is capable of bringing about this conversion, or may be used to do so.

There is something to be said for each of these attempts at justification, but it may be argued that each, taken by itself, is to some extent inadequate. If, according to one version of 'utilitarian', justification is given strictly in terms of usefulness, this would be an indictment of what is now generally accepted as a curriculum, since much of what is included in it would not seem to be particularly useful in the ordinary sense of the word. Trigonometry, knowledge of the policies of the Plantagenet kings, or of the causes of the Trade Winds, are not all that useful for the average citizen who would get on very well without them. Most teachers, however, would want to include knowledge of this kind in the curriculum even though it might not seem 'useful' in any ordinary, mundane sense. This follows from a conviction that education should involve the acquisition of some knowledge 'for its own sake' apart from any direct or immediate usefulness it may have for the learner. The more particular, hedonistic Utilitarian version, which bases its justification on the production of happiness, seems suspect in that it is likely that education, as structured by the traditional curriculum, does not on the whole, or necessarily, tend to increase a man's happiness or make him a source of happiness to others. Indeed, by making him more aware of and sensitive to the human condition it may only succeed in making him less contented than before. Moreover, it may be argued that happiness depends so much on the general circumstances of a man's life that education is able to do very little about it so far as individuals are concerned, and to try to justify a curriculum as a means to happiness is to claim more for it than the facts warrant.

The 'rational mind' type of justification, whilst it has the merit of seeing education in terms of human improvement, as tending towards rationality and autonomy, is perhaps open to the objection that it leans too far away from what was, after all, acceptable in the utilitarian case. It tends to emphasise the 'understanding', aspect without necessarily emphasising the need to make sure that what is taught is, in a mundane sense, useful to the learner. It would be possible to give a rational understanding, to make a rational mind, through mathematics and science, art and religion, by concentrating on aspects of those subjects which had little practical application to everyday life. [17 chapter 4] Initiation into algebra, astronomy and the arguments involved in dogmatic theology would no doubt make for rationality, but would not be particularly useful to men in general. Much the same kind of reservations might be held concerning the 'heritage' approach which, whilst it meets the requirement that knowledge should be seen as important in its own right, as part of the human culture, may sometimes seem to be concerned with issues remote from everyday practical affairs.

The fact is that each of these attempted justifications calls attention in turn to an important aspect of the curriculum, although none of them will suffice entirely on its own. An adequate justification would involve what is sound in each of these three approaches. Utility, or plain usefulness, may not be the only warrant for what is taught, but it is true that unless what is taught is likely to be useful to the learner, or tends towards happiness generally, its inclusion in the curriculum would be at least questionable. Then again, if it can be shown that a subject is a means of giving a child an increasingly rational grasp of the nature of reality, or is a way of introducing him to an appreciation and understanding of his cultural heritage, this would be a strong consideration in its favour and do much to offset any lack of direct or immediate usefulness. The curriculum may thus be partly and to some extent justified in a number of ways: that what it provides is directly useful, or tends on the whole to increase happiness, or underwrites rationality in the conduct of affairs, or does something to make the learner a civilised human being, aware of and appreciative of what is distinctive in human culture. A subject or discipline which met all these criteria would be a prime candidate for inclusion; those which fell short in one respect or other would need to have a special case made for their inclusion.

## 5 Conclusion

This chapter set out to review briefly the answers to two important questions: what is knowledge? and: what knowledge is of most worth? The answer to the first question introduced two possible paradigms of knowledge: formal knowledge, such as is to be found in mathematics and logic, and empirical knowledge, which constitutes the various sciences. Each of these possible paradigms has tempted philosophers to claim that it alone is *the* paradigm. The history of philosophy reveals many attempts to show that all 'true' knowledge is either mathematical or scientific in character. More recently, however, it has been recognised that it is unrealistic to restrict knowledge to one or two paradigms, that there are several distinct 'forms' of knowledge, each with its own structure and testing procedures. On this view, in addition to mathematics and science, morals are a form of knowledge, as are also aesthetics and religion, and these various forms may be combined to constitute composite 'fields' of knowledge, geography, architecture, and medicine, for example. The position taken up on this point will influence one's views of the curriculum. Those educators who have tended to regard knowledge largely in terms of the mathematical paradigm have tended to emphasise the importance of formal studies and a deductive pedagogy.

Empiricists have tended to envisage it largely in terms of science, with an associated pedagogy of discovery and experiment. Recognition of the essentially plural nature of knowledge gives a more flexible and diversified version of the curriculum, in which each discipline is seen to be distinct and autonomous, with its own characteristic methods and procedures.

Answers to the second question raise a consideration of values and link curriculum theory with a general theory of education. A general theory, as was argued in chapter 2, makes an assumption about a worthwhile end to be achieved. The question then is: what knowledge is most calculated to bring about the kind of person specified in the aim, the educated man? Various answers may be given: useful knowledge, knowledge likely to promote happiness, knowledge required to produce a rational mind, knowledge which turns a human animal into a human being. The answer given will indicate an attempt to justify a curriculum, since the curriculum is a means to the desired end. This chapter suggests that all these answers are acceptable to some extent and that taken together they provide an adequate justification of the traditional curriculum.

## Suggestions for further reading

There is a vast literature on the nature of knowledge, much of it technical and difficult for a beginner in philosophy. A good introduction is I. Scheffler, *Conditions of Knowledge* (Scott, Foresman, 1965). D.W. Hamlyn, *The Theory of Knowledge* (Macmillan, 1970), chapters 4 and 5, is more difficult. See also A.J. Ayer, *The Problem of Knowledge*, chapter 1, and

G. Ryle, *The Concept of Mind*, chapter 2, for a 'linguistic' approach to this topic.

Writings on the curriculum are also considerable in volume. Hirst and Peters give a good philosophical introduction in *The Logic of Education*, chapter 4. See also P.H. Hirst, *Knowledge and the Curriculum*. The historical theorists of education, Plato, Rousseau, Mill, Dewey *et al.*, all embody theories of the curriculum in their texts. An interesting and readable justification of the traditional curriculum is given by H. Spencer, in 'What Knowledge is of Most Worth?' included in *Education*. A cogently argued philosophical point of view is J.P. White, *Towards a Compulsory Curriculum* (Routledge & Kegan Paul, 1973). The paper by M. Oakeshott, 'Education: The Engagement and its Frustration' in *Education and the Development of Reason*, is a plea for the liberal curriculum.

# 4     Teaching and educating

## 1 Introduction

It has been maintained in this book so far that education is an enterprise which aims at producing a certain
type of person and that this is accomplished by the
transmission of knowledge, skills and understanding
from one person to another. The philosopher's role is
seen as being that of scrutinising the various assumptions and justifications made and offered by practitioners and theorists in this field. We have, consequently,
examined in an elementary way notions like educational
aims and purposes, the nature of educational theorising
and the nature of knowledge. We need now to look at
the 'transmission' aspect of education. The curriculum
sets out *what* is to be taught and, once again, raises
implicitly the question of justification. Transmission
involves pedagogy and this in turn raises questions of
clarification and justification. We are now to be concerned not so much with what is taught but with how
it is taught, with the concepts of teaching and training
and with the associated issue of indoctrination. In
examining these topics we shall need to deal with the
roles and positions of both teacher and pupil and with
the extent to which teaching and educating involves
the concepts of authority, discipline and punishment.

## 2 'Teaching' and 'educating'

Teaching is obviously closely connected with, if not absolutely necessary to, education. Whether or not education could go on in its absence is debatable, but in practice teaching is central to the enterprise. The concept of teaching, however, is by no means an easy one to handle. For one thing, the word 'teaching' is not the name of any one activity. Teaching may involve many different kinds of activities: talking, asking questions, writing on a blackboard, setting up situations in which pupils can learn, and many others. It is often difficult to draw the line which separates teaching from other activities which may resemble it. For example, is giving information teaching? Is punishing a child a form of teaching? Does a teacher teach by his manner, his way of life, his example? Is dressing conventionally or unconventionally a kind of teaching? Can one teach unintentionally, by accident? These are not unimportant questions. A teacher will properly be held responsible for his teaching and so it is as well to be clear about what counts as teaching and what does not. The analysis given in this section will point to two conclusions. Firstly, that teaching necessarily involves the intention that someone should learn as a result of what one does; secondly, that teaching requires a recognition by both teacher and pupil of a special relationship existing between them.

Teaching is an intentional matter. To teach is to intend that someone should learn something. [7 chapter 5] If this intention is lacking, then whatever the agent is doing — acting, entertaining, amusing himself — he is not engaged in teaching although he may perhaps be

67

pretending to be. Of course, it is not necessary that the pupil should as a matter of fact learn anything. Teaching need not be successful. But if the teacher sets about his task in a way appropriate to the occasion, appropriate that is to the age and abilities of his pupils, with the intention that they should learn something, then to that extent he is teaching. This means that although one can teach but be unsuccessful, one can't teach by accident, or unintentionally. It may be that the pupil will learn something that the teacher does not intend him to learn. He may learn something from the teacher's accent, or his demeanour, or his style of dressing, but it does not follow from this that the teacher *taught* him to speak or behave or dress in a certain way. One can learn without being taught. An unsympathetic or bad-tempered teacher does not 'teach' a child to dislike history or mathematics, although the child may come to dislike the subject simply because he dislikes the teacher. He learns to dislike the subject but he has not been taught to do so. Teaching has taken place when what is learnt is learnt as a result of someone's deliberate intention.

A qualification needs to be made here concerning the contention above that teaching does not have to be successful. In general this is so. A teacher may teach throughout a whole afternoon, intending that his pupils should learn, but be defeated by their laziness, or tiredness or by some extraneous influence, noise or confusion. In this case he could properly be said to have been teaching, although unsuccessfully, as one can properly be said to have spent the whole afternoon fishing although nothing was caught. There is, however, a sense of 'teach' in which the notion of success is implied. I can hardly be said to have taught a boy to swim unless he actually learns to swim as a result of my efforts. This complication comes about because the word 'teach' has both a 'task' and an 'achievement' sense. If the word is used, as it generally is, in its 'task' sense, then success is not implied in its use. We may fail at a task. If it is used as an 'achievement' word then the notion of a successful outcome is part of its meaning.

The second point to be made here is that to teach is to set up and recognise, however minimally, a special relationship between one person and another, teacher and pupil. A teacher is one who intends to make himself responsible for someone's learning, and commits himself to take pains to see that the knowledge is acquired, to vary his methods if necessary to bring this learning about. A teacher, as such, assumes a responsibility towards his pupil. This recognition of responsibility is essential to the existence of a teaching situation. For a teaching situation to exist there must also be a recognition by the pupil that he too is in a special relationship with another, that it is his responsibility to pay attention, to try to understand what is being done, to enter into a joint enterprise. These recognitions need be no more than minimal. They are compatible with laziness and naughtiness on the part of the pupil and with laziness and incompetence on the part of the teacher. But so long as there is this minimal recognition of their relationship, of what *ought* to be going on, teaching is taking place, however ineffectively, however badly. This dual requirement of intention and a recognition of a special responsibility on both sides is what distinguishes a genuine teaching situation from one in which one party merely gives information to another. The announcer at Victoria Station does not teach passengers about their trains. He tells them, gives them information. He intends that they should learn some facts, but there is no recognition on either side of the special relationship that characterises a teaching situation. The announcer is not a teacher, nor is the passenger a pupil.

Teaching, it was said earlier, is connected closely with education but the connection is, on one side at least, a contingent one only. We may teach all sorts of things, good or bad, error as well as truth, bad manners as well as good. We may teach children to be truthful and honest or, like Fagin, teach them to lie or steal. We may teach them truths which are trivial and which no one never needs to know. Education, however, involves teaching what is worth knowing and attitudes which are morally acceptable. Not all teaching need amount to educating. Moreover there is, in the normative concept of education, the implication that the methods used are morally acceptable. This is not so in the case of teaching. Teaching would still be teaching, given the two criteria mentioned above, intention and recognition of responsibility, even if the methods used were harsh or immoral. It does not follow from the fact that someone is teaching, and teaching effectively, that education is going on, although it would generally be the case that if education is taking place some teaching is being done by somebody. Education involves the transmission of knowledge and skills, and it is difficult to see how this could happen in practice unless someone makes himself responsible for the transmission. Of course, teaching need not be of the obvious, didactic kind, with one person telling another what is the case, or what ought to be done. It might very well take the negative form recommended by Rousseau in *Emile*, where the pupil is encouraged to find out for himself. But in so far as this was an educational situation there would have to be some intervention by the teacher, giving a rationale for what was being done. In the special case of 'self-education' the roles of teacher and pupil are shared by the same person, but the teacher's role is there nonetheless. We may sum all this up by using some technical terms of philosophy and say that teaching may be a necessary condition of education taking place but is not a sufficient condition. Education usually involves teaching, but not all teaching need be educative and some of it is not.

## 3 'Training' and 'indoctrination'

These two terms bear a resemblance to the two dealt with in the previous section. 'Training' seems to be analogous to 'teaching' and indeed may be substituted for it in some circumstances. 'Indoctrination' seems analogous to 'education' but with the reservation that whereas 'education' carries overtones of approval, 'indoctrination' usually has a pejorative sense.

The term 'training' is usually used in those situations where some skill or competence is involved, often, though not always, where the skill is fairly limited in scope. [16 chapter 1] We talk about training animals to perform tricks and of training soldiers to operate their equipment. But we also talk of training teachers and lawyers and doctors, where the range of activities is by no means limited in scope. Perhaps the best interpretation is that training entails providing learners with a range of strategies and tactics which will enable them to operate successfully within a given field of activity. A trained fireman is one who knows what to do at the scene of a fire, and a trained lawyer is one who is able to act expertly when presented with a legal problem. The connection with teaching is then straightforward. Trainees have to be taught the competences required and be given opportunities to exercise their newly acquired skills. Plainly, training can take place in circumstances where no one would claim that education was going on. To train a soldier in the use of a bayonet or a gas mask is hardly to educate him. The training of firemen, airline pilots or footballers seems to have little if anything to do with their education. 'Highly trained but uneducated' would not appear to be a contradiction in terms. Yet it would be wrong to suppose that there can be no connections between the two. There is no reason why training should not, in some circumstances, be educative. A training programme which involved not only giving skills of a particular kind, but also the giving to the trainee of some insight into different modes of thinking, an awareness of the interconnections of the various kinds of knowledge involved and a concern for the intellectual virtues of accuracy and respect for evidence, would to that extent be educative. Teachers and lawyers, for example, could very well be given an education during their course of training and modern institutions for legal training and teacher training properly aim at doing this.

'Indoctrination' seems to have close connections with 'teaching' and 'training' in that the implication is in each case that the pupil or the learner is being manipulated in some way by an interested party. In so far as the manipulation is directed towards some end regarded as desirable by the manipulator it has some analogy with education. There is, however, very little agreement amongst philosophers of education as to what constitutes indoctrination in practice. Some have seen it as a form of teaching which relies heavily on authoritarian methods and which seeks to establish in the learner beliefs and attitudes which subsequent experience will not change. Some have wanted to deny that it is a form of teaching at all, on the grounds that teaching involves a willingness on the part of the teacher to submit his teaching to rational criticism from the pupil, which the indoctrinator as such is generally reluctant to do. [23] Some have shifted the emphasis from the intention of the indoctrinator to the subject matter he wishes to transmit to the learner. Indoctrination, it is said, is a matter of *what* is taught, indoctrination taking place when beliefs which are themselves open to question are taught as though they were not so. Perhaps the least contentious account would be that indoctrination is a form of teaching in which it is intended that certain beliefs should be accepted without question, either because it is thought that they are not only important but unquestionably true, or because, for various reasons, it is thought important that, true or not, they should not be questioned. Those who hold firm religious convictions might support indoctrination on the first count, and those who subscribe to certain sorts of political opinions might do so on the second. It is doubtful, however, whether indoctrination could ever amount to education in its normative sense, since this presupposes that the learner should be initiated into practices involving rational procedures. Indoctrination is typically non-rational in temper, non-rational in the sense that it requires certain conclusions to be put beyond the scope of critical enquiry. [24]

## 4 Education as 'transaction' or 'discovery'

In chapter 2 a distinction was made between two different approaches to a general theory of education, a distinction between a mechanistic and an organic approach, based upon different assumptions about the nature of man. On the one hand, there was the assumption that man is analogous to a machine, a system of inputs and outputs, whose outputs or behaviours could be shaped and directed from without. On the other hand, the assumption was that man is essentially an organism, growing and developing from within, whose development could be facilitated by the provision of congenial and stimulating environments. This distinction translates into different notions or theories about the role of the teacher and of his pupil.

The mechanistic approach, in its simplest form, sees education as a transaction between teacher and pupil, in which, initially at least, all the advantages are on one side and all the shortcomings on the other. The teacher is an authority, a repository of knowledge, an expert. The pupil is none of these. The transaction takes the form of the teacher handing over to the pupil the knowledge and the skills he needs. There is a one-way flow, from teacher to pupil, since only in this way can advantage occur. The teacher has little if anything to learn from the pupil; the pupil has everything to learn from the teacher. Thus the situation calls for maximum pedagogical activity by the teacher and maximum receptivity from the pupil. It is the recognition of these roles by both parties which makes a teaching situation possible. The teacher's business is to maximise the pupil's inputs, to devise the means of making those associations in the pupil's mind which constitute knowledge, understanding and skill. It is the pupil's task to receive the inputs, to do his best to make the appropriate associations. Pupil activity is, ideally, limited to the tasks designed to make those associations. 'Free' or 'unstructured' activity is to be deprecated, especially that involving pupils with one another, play for example, or collaboration. The teacher's role is thus primarily didactic and regulatory. He provides the material, organises the making of associations, and checks whether such associations are made. His aim is to achieve the desired outputs from the pupil, the right sort of behaviour.

The organic approach tends to weaken the rigid polarity which characterises the mechanistic model. The 'transaction' aspect diminishes and emphasis is thrown on the pupil's need to develop his own methods of working and acquiring knowledge and skill. The teacher may still be regarded as an authority, but his role will not be didactic or expository so much as that of a supervisor or consultant. His place will be on the fringes of the various activities which go on in the classroom. He will be ready with advice and help but not too ready to play the schoolmaster and make his presence felt. The centre of maximum activity will be the pupil himself. Ideally he will be engaged in activities which exercise his capacities and stimulate his interests, and his task will be to make sense of his environment and build up for himself an accurate picture of reality. This he will be encouraged to do by exploration, by experiment, by trial and error, by insight, through dealing with the concrete reality presented to him. Education will be not so much a transaction as a process of discovery. The textbook will be less important than here-and-now problems to be solved. Moreover, there will be no point in restricting the pupil's attention to the words of the teacher, since it is not the primary task of the teacher to give information or to tell the child what to do. There will be advantages in a lateral polarity, between pupil and pupil, so that they can learn from one another. Pupils will be encouraged to cooperate with each other, to acquire the benefits and disciplines of mutual toleration in a common task. The social discipline of cooperation will tend to replace the regulatory role of the teacher. Behind all this is the notion that the individual's education is proceeding from within, as a growing realisation of his place and predicament comes to him from his attempts to discover the nature of his world through his own efforts.

## 5 Participation and authority

The distinction between the mechanistic and the organic approaches to education and the associated distinction between education as a transaction or a process of discovery enable us to look more closely at the different roles of teacher and pupil. Education is concerned with the schooling and improvement of the pupil and this depends on the participation of the pupil in what is going on. The kind of pupil participation involved will be governed to a large extent by the way in which the educator sees the educative process. If the teacher adopts the mechanistic assumption that the child is a kind of empty vessel, to be filled up with intellectual goods, then the pupil's participation will very likely be restricted, so far as possible, to the passive role of listening to his teacher, receiving information, imitating and emulating the teacher's example. His participation will be individualistic in that it will require particular responses made by him alone to demands made on his attention. If the teacher takes the organic view, that children are developing, exploring creatures, the pupil's participation will be organised to take a different form. His role will be that of cooperator with his fellows in joint enterprises in the classroom, in the course of which enterprises knowledge and skills and understanding are acquired.

What is philosophically important here is the conceptual point that whatever general theory of education informs actual practice in the classroom, the pupil's role is essentially that of participant. This conclusion comes from our understanding of the nature of education in its normative sense. If education is the intentional initiation of a pupil into areas of knowledge, skill and understanding, pupil participation is not only a practical necessity but a logical one also. It is a practical necessity because unless the pupil takes some interest, however slight, in what is going on no education is likely to take place. It is also a logical necessity because no one can be initiated into anything unless he himself takes a part in the process of initiation. Initiation doesn't simply happen to one, like catching a cold. It involves a deliberate recognition of a process in which one is engaged. To be educated involves one in a recognition of the part one is playing. This recognition, like that required to establish a teaching situation, need only be minimal, but if education is to take place at all some recognition, some participation, must occur. Unless the pupil admits himself to be, to some extent, a part of the proceedings, with a responsibility to take notice, to pay attention, to try to understand what is going on, no teaching situation exists, and certainly not an educational situation. In order to be a pupil a child must be a participator. He may be so reluctantly, with backslidings, but in so far as he is a pupil he must, to a minimal degree, take part. The pupil's role, as pupil, is simply this: a participator in a process designed to teach him and perhaps to educate him. Different theories of education define the form which his logically necessary participation may take in practice.

The other participant is the teacher. The form of his participation will also depend on the educational theory adopted. A mechanistic type of educational theory will embrace the teacher as an authority, conveying knowledge and skills by giving his pupils such experiences as are likely to produce correct associations of ideas, by modifying their responses to serve some desired end. His participation in the enterprise will be a matter of shaping the pupil's behaviour from without. An organic, child-centred theory will tend to avoid the strict polarity between teacher and pupil, and see the teacher's participation as being largely that of giving advice and supervision. The teacher will be concerned mainly with the arrangement of the environment, to enable the pupil to engage in activities which interest him and which will allow him to develop his capacities and 'grow' as a person. The teacher's role, as participant, is weaker than with the mechanistic approach. This follows from what has been called the 'horticultural metaphor', the assumption that the child 'grows' or develops to maturity as a plant does. The teacher's role is thereby assimilated to that of a gardener who tends a plant. [5] A gardener can do no more than attend the process of growth. He may accelerate it, possibly, or train it in one direction or another, but he can't enter into it in any way. A plant has to do its own growing, from within. So, it is argued, a teacher may be able to speed up the growth of the pupil, or direct it, but he can't teach the pupil to grow or develop. All he can do is to 'help the child learn'. This has led some advocates of the organic, child-centred theories to deprecate any substantial intervention by the teacher into the child's affairs, on the grounds that this imposition of adult values in an area which is not adult is likely to hinder or thwart the natural 'growth' of the child.

There are certain shortcomings in this horticultural metaphor if it is imported into educational theory. One objection to it is that its adoption tends to reduce the teacher's responsibility for his pupil's education. If education were simply a matter of growth, in the way that the history of a plant is a matter of growth, the teacher's role might well be no more than standing by and preserving a congenial environment. But the end of education is not simply a fully grown man but an educated man, and to educate more is needed than a watchful tending of the environment. To educate, the teacher has to see that the pupil's mind is structured, that he has the proper conceptual apparatus, that he knows how to use what he has learned. To educate, a teacher must intervene in his pupil's career in ways for which there is no analogy in the case of the gardener and the plant. The teacher is responsible for the education of his pupil and this means that he must take up more than a merely supervisory, sideline stance. As was indicated in the section on teaching, the teacher must see himself as in a special relationship with his pupil, that of being responsible for getting him to learn what he needs to learn. Moreover, it is crucial to the teacher's role as educator that he should be an authority, so far as the pupil is concerned, on what he teaches. This is, again, where the 'gardener' metaphor is misleading. The gardener certainly needs to be an authority or an expert on those matters which concern the nurture of the plant and the proper conditions for its growth. The teacher also has to be an authority in an analogous sense. He needs to know about those material and psychological considerations which are best suited to educational progress. But he needs to be more than this. He also has to be an authority in respect of those elements which constitute the growth of the child's mind, the knowledge, skills and attitudes which make up that restructuring of experience which Dewey calls 'growth'. The gardener cannot structure the plant's development by any exercise of authority or knowledge. The teacher *has* to do this for his pupil. This structuring of the child's mind involves the exercise of academic authority, and this, like the notion of participation, is a logical point. It is, of course, possible to *teach* what one doesn't know; it is possible to teach error. But to *educate* involves in the cognitive sphere at least, teaching the pupil what is worth knowing, and what is worth knowing must, as a matter of logic, be true. So as a logical condition of being an educator the teacher must participate as an authority. Unless he is an authority he can't be an educator.

The practice of education, then, involves at least a minimum degree of participation by both pupil and teacher. Teaching and educating are enterprises in which both parties have to commit themselves to some extent: the teacher commits himself to monitor the pupil's learning and to make himself responsible for it, and also to see that what is learned is worth learning. The pupil commits himself to submission to the authority of the teacher and also to take some pains to enter into the spirit of the enterprise. Finally, the enterprise requires that the teacher should be an authority on what he teaches since unless he is so he is in no logical position to enter into that structuring of the pupil's mind which constitutes education.

## 6 Authority and discipline

So far one aspect of the teacher as authority has been dealt with, that is, his role as an authority on what he teaches, one in possession of knowledge and skills which he will try to transmit to pupils. There is, of course, another sense in which a teacher may be regarded as an authority: his capacity to be in charge of what goes on in the classroom. It is this aspect of the teacher's job which shows up most dramatically when this capacity is lacking. Traditionally the teacher has been regarded as one who should keep order in his class and see that the external conditions obtain in which teaching and educating can be carried on. A competent teacher is one who is able to maintain 'discipline'. As with all the concepts with which the philosopher of education is concerned, the concept of discipline is complex and needs a certain amount of disentangling. The root notion here is that of 'order'. To maintain discipline is to maintain some degree of order, and this implies some degree of restraint or constraint. Subjects like mathematics and science are called 'disciplines', partly at least because there is the implication that in studying them one is not free to do as one pleases. They require submission to logical or empirical limitations. Similarly, a state of discipline implies that behaviour is subject to limitations, to rules and order. Part of the teacher's task is to set limits to his pupil's activities, to maintain discipline in his class. There is more than one way in which he may do this. He may be able to frighten his pupil into obedience and orderliness by threats, or secure these by the use of physical force. The traditional teacher who figures in educational folklore was generally supposed to maintain discipline in this way. Another way, recommended or suggested by John Dewey, is to rely on the internal discipline of the group; the idea here being that if pupils are jointly engaged in some occupation which interests them the requirements of the collective task will impose an order on them, and recalcitrant members of the group will be disciplined by their fellows. [3 chapter 4] A more sophisticated account and one connected with, and usually confused with, the notion that discipline involves frightening the pupil, is that the teacher maintains discipline by the exercise of his authority. The confusion comes from the tendency to identify authority with the use of force and the inculcation of fear. To avoid this confusion we need to look more closely at the concept of the teacher 'in authority'.

Authority, in this sense of taking charge, may be a matter of form or fact, or both. Formal authority,

authority *de jure*, is authority given as a consequence of one's place in a system of rules and conventions. An army officer, a policeman, a magistrate, a teacher, all have authority *de jure* by virtue of their appointment. They are given the right to obedience in their respective spheres. Authority *de facto*, authority in practice, is simply the ability to get one's orders obeyed. These two kinds of authority are only contingently connected. A policeman or a teacher may have authority *de jure* but be quite ineffective in action, in the face of an unruly crowd or an unruly class. On the other hand there have been charismatic characters like Jesus or Joan of Arc who have been able to get others to obey them although they themselves had no formal authority to rely upon. Ideally, of course, those who have authority *de jure* also have authority *de facto*, but this is not necessarily the case. What is central to the notion of authority is being able to get orders obeyed simply by giving them. Thus the exercise of authority *de facto* rules out other ways of securing obedience. It rules out the use of bribery, importunity, and deception, and it rules out the use of threats or force. If people do as they are told simply because they are scared or because they are threatened this is not the exercise of authority. It is the use of force, actual or threatened, and this is no more the exercise of authority than deceiving them or appealing to their better natures would be. Authority *de facto* consists in getting obedience without resorting to these alternatives. It is usually the case that anyone in formal authority will have at his disposal some force or sanction which he may use. But the use of force, or the threat of doing so, is a sign that authority *de facto* has broken down. It is when people do not do as they are ordered that threats have to be made or actual force used, and the purpose of threatening or using force is to restore authority if this is possible, or, failing that, to restore order and discipline. When force is used this is simply a recognition that authority *de facto* is gone and all that remains is authority *de jure* which, by itself, is useless. Authority *de jure* which fails in practice requires the use of force as an alternative to authority *de facto*. Authority is one thing, the use of force is quite another; they are connected but they are not the same. Clarity demands that they should not be confused with one another.[16 chapter 9]


## 7 Authority and punishment

When force is used formally by those in authority it is usually referred to as punishment. Here again we have a concept relevant to educational issues which is complex and requires some clarification. The root notion in punishment is that it requires the intentional infliction of pain on someone who has committed an offence. This infliction of pain must, strictly, be undertaken by someone who has been given a right to do so, someone in authority *de jure*. Moreover, the pain must follow as a consequence of the offence. These various requirements or criteria are, however, susceptible to some variation. Strictly, a punishment can only be inflicted on an offender. It has a retributive function. But it is possible to weaken this requirement to allow for the fact that we do sometimes talk of 'innocent' people being 'punished'. In this case we would talk of 'unwarranted' or 'unjustified' punishment. We may sometimes allow that punishment may be given by someone not in authority, a passer-by, for example, who metes out 'punishment' to a misbehaving child. Here we would talk of 'unauthorised' punishment. When the defining criteria are varied in this way we still talk of 'punishment' but recognise that we are using a weakened version of the term. When all the criteria are complied with we have the paradigm sense of 'punishment', punishment on a juridical model. This requires essentially that authority should be involved in what is done, authority *de jure*, that is.

The concepts of authority, discipline and punishment are closely bound up with the business of teaching and educating. Education implies the transmitting of knowledge and skills by one who is an authority to those who are not. To enable this to take place certain external conditions must obtain. The pupil must be reasonably orderly and attentive, and the instructions of the teacher must generally be obeyed. So to be effective the teacher needs not only to be an authority on what he teaches but also to function in authority. He will normally have authority *de jure* consequent upon his appointment; he needs also to have authority *de facto* since if he does not his classroom is likely to be chaos. Ideally he should maintain discipline by the exercise of his authority *de facto*. How far he can do this will depend on his personality, his rapprochement with his pupils and the extent to which he has mastered the arts of class management. When, as may happen, his authority is challenged he may have to resort to punishment. Punishment would then be justified as a means of restoring the position which existed before the offence took place. Three points arising out of this may be made here.

Firstly, punishment would be justified in this case since the conditions of a juridical situation would be present: there would have been an offence, and punishment would perhaps do something to prevent a repetition of the offence. It does not mean, however, that punishment would necessarily be the best way of dealing with the situation. It simply means that punishment would not be ruled out as juridically inappropriate. The second point is that referred to earlier in more general terms, that is, when discipline breaks down and punishment has to be used this is an admission that authority *de facto* has been lost. This is particularly so if the punishment involves the use of physical force, but it is also true when punishment takes milder forms such as the giving of impositions and detentions. In all these cases conformity is being sought by means other than the exercise of authority *de facto*. It may be argued that punishment is being used to restore this lost authority, but the truth of this is questionable. If pupils come to order because of the punishment or because of the fear of punishment, it is no longer the exercise of authority which disciplines them but simply the use of force. It could well be argued that punishment used in this way does little if anything to restore authority. At best it restores the *status quo*, and it may not be the best way of doing this.

The third point is that punishment, although connected with teaching, should not itself be regarded as a kind of teaching. Teaching involves the transmission of knowledge and skill and implies activities like the giving of explanations and reasons. A child may learn something as the result of a punishment, for example that he will be punished if he comes late, or is insolent or disorderly, but the punishment as such does not teach him this. The mere infliction of pain conveys no new information. Some teaching, about rules and expectations, has to precede or go alongside the punishment if the punishment is to make sense to the child. Punishment may be administered by the teacher, as authority, but teaching is one thing, punishment another. [13]

## 8 Conclusion

This chapter has dealt with a group of related concepts which have to do with the actual business of educating. They belong to pedagogy, that part of a general theory of education which comes under the heading of 'assumptions about methods'. For education to go on at all someone must learn something, and this generally will involve someone else in teaching. To do this, the teacher, in so far as he is educating, has to be in a logically superior position to his pupils: he needs to know more than they do. No one can educate another unless he is an authority compared with his pupils. The pupil, in order to be a pupil in anything other than name, must regard himself as being in a certain relationship with his teacher, as one who is committed to paying attention and trying to learn. It is not suggested that this commitment need be more than minimal, but some such commitment there must be. This mutual recognition of a teacher-pupil relationship is the basis of discipline, which in an educational context requires a degree of submission and restraint in the interests of learning. The teacher's role in this relationship is that of being *in* authority, as one who has a right to be

87

obeyed, as distinct from his right, as an authority on what he teaches, to be listened to. The exercise of authority maintains the regime in which education can effectively take place. When authority fails in practice the regime may need to be preserved by the use of punishment or the threat of it. When authority fails education is put at risk, and this fact constitutes such justification as there is for punishment in schools.

Thus, teaching, training, the exercise of authority, discipline and punishment depend for their justification on the extent to which they facilitate that initiation into worthwhile goods which constitutes education. Authority, however, may sometimes be carried to abuse. When it is exercised simply for its own sake it degenerates into authoritarianism, a form of tyranny. Where it is used to inhibit criticism it becomes indoctrination, tyranny of another kind.

These conclusions apply whichever of the two main approaches to educational theory is adopted. The differences between the mechanistic or 'traditional' approach and the more organic or 'progressive' approach will often be no more than differences in emphasis. In either case education demands participation by both pupil and teacher. In each case there must be assumed a corpus of knowledge which it is desirable that the pupil should acquire, and an assumption about the external conditions in which the knowledge may be most effectively acquired. The two approaches may perhaps best be understood as each drawing attention to different aspects of a whole, which is the practice of education: the one emphasising the necessary requirements of knowledge and effort and the discipline required to make the practice effective, the other emphasising the equally important truth that education is nothing if not a process of individual growth and development.

## Suggestions for further reading

An analysis of the concept of teaching is offered in P.H. Hirst and R.S. Peters, *The Logic of Education*, chapters 5 and 6. Other useful articles are by G. Ryle, 'Teaching and Training', I. Scheffler, 'Philosophical Models of Teaching', and M. Oakeshott, 'Learning and Teaching', all in *The Concept of Education* (ed. R.S. Peters, Routledge & Kegan Paul, 1967). Also in this volume, J.P. White's 'Indoctrination' is a good introduction to this topic. A more extended treatment of indoctrination is I.A. Snook, *Indoctrination and Education*.

A brief discussion of the relationship between authority and participation in education is given in the chapter by T.W. Moore and D. Lawton, in *The Theory and Practice of Curriculum Studies* (eds. Lawton *et al.*, Routledge & Kegan Paul, 1978). The nature of authority and its implications for education is dealt with at some length in R.S. Peters, *Ethics and Education*, chapter 9. Punishment and education is discussed in chapter 10 of this work. Punishment and its relevance to education is also dealt with by T.W. Moore, 'Punishment and Education', in *Proceedings of Philosophy of Education Society of Great Britain*, vol. 1, 1966, and by P.M. Moore and P.S. Wilson in *Proceedings of the Society*, vol. VIII, no. 1 (1974).

# 5 Education, morals and religion

## 1 Introduction

It is generally held that there is a close connection between education and morals and between education and religion. Indeed, many people in the past believed, although perhaps not so many would do so today, that the whole point of education lies in its moralising and religious force. Dr Arnold, the headmaster of Rugby, believed it to be the business of the public school to turn out Christian gentlemen. Cardinal Newman in his *Discourses on university teaching* emphasised the integral part which religious studies must play, as he saw it, in any system of liberal education. The great significance given to religious teaching in this country is reflected in the provision that such teaching should be regarded as compulsory in all schools covered by the Education Act of 1944. The assumption that education should be concerned with the moral life of the pupil is one that few teachers and parents would care to contest. In its strongest form the conviction would be that moral and religious teaching are essential to education, in that education is not really possible without them. We may note here that such a view would constitute a theory *about* education, that is, the theory that education necessarily involves a religious and moral content. It is such a theory which prescribes that in all state schools in this country the day should include some form of corporate worship, and which convinces many teachers that they have an obligation, as teachers, to further the moral training and religious beliefs of their pupils. The philosopher of education may point out here that such a theory may rest on, and derive its plausibility from, a stipulative use of the term 'education', whereby the inclusion of a moral and religious element is made a part of the meaning of the term. Whether or not this is a useful move to make will be examined briefly in this chapter, which takes a philosophical look at the theory, to test its credentials as a theory of education.

## 2 Morals and education

Morals, or morality, have to do with human behaviour judged from a normative point of view. It is about what ought to be done, as distinct from what is in fact done. We may distinguish morals from prudential considerations, which are about what ought to be done primarily in the interests of the person doing the action. Prudence concerns those duties we owe primarily to ourselves. Morality is about those actions which affect the interests and well-being of others, as well as ourselves.

About the whole field of moral studies we may make the point which in our first chapter we made about education itself. We may think of morals as being concerned with a hierarchy of activities. At the lowest logical level there are moral practices, like telling the truth, keeping promises and paying debts. At a logically higher level there are moral theories, which try to give a general account of, or a justification of, conclusions about what ought to be done in practice. Moral theories like Utilitarianism, Intuitionism and Emotivism belong at this level. At a higher level still comes the analysis of concepts and the scrutiny of moral theories which constitutes moral philosophy. The moral philosopher is concerned with the actual usage of moral language, with concepts like 'good' and 'right' and 'duty', and with the validity and acceptability of theories which are offered to justify moral decisions and judgments. That there will be a connection between the findings of the moral theorist, the moral philosopher and the philosopher of education is very likely, the more so if education is regarded as a predominantly 'moral' enterprise. But the precise connection between morals and education and the degree to which they are connected are not at all easy to establish. There is, in fact, some reason to suppose that the study of education in the past has been somewhat overmoralised, and that some educational theorists and philosophers of education have been led far deeper into the complicated labyrinths of moral theory than has been strictly necessary. This is not to deny that the moral philosopher has some important insights to give to the educator and to the philosopher of education. It is simply to say that moral philosophy is a wide and still inadequately charted ocean and that the philosopher of education must be careful not to get lost on it.

Granted, then, that morals have something important to do with education, we may ask: what is the connection between them? This is itself a philosophical enquiry. Is the connection a necessary one, that is, logically necessary, in that morals are essential to education? Or is the connection merely contingent, in that education may, and does, as a matter of fact, include some moral content?

The view that morals and education are necessarily connected springs partly from the belief that education is the initiation of a pupil into areas of knowledge and understanding which are themselves valuable. Education is a normative matter. The implication here, more often stated than argued, is that the value, or worthwhileness, involved is a moral quality, so that when one is teaching mathematics or science or history one is serving a moral end. A strong version of this view is that the real value of these disciplines comes from their moral content, that what is important in them is the concern for truth, order and discipline, which are categorised as elements of morality. If this were so, then the whole of education would be informed with morality and to talk about education apart from morality would be a contradiction in terms. This, however, seems to overstate the case. We may agree that to be educative what is taught must be something of value, something worth learning, but this is not to say that the subjects themselves must be worth-while in any positive moral sense. Many of the traditional academic disciplines are in fact morally neutral. Their value consists in their being useful to the learner, or as involving worthwhile considerations of a non-moral kind. A concern for truth, in the sense of accuracy, correctness, and a respect for evidence, elegance and economy, are not as such to do with moral values. They have more in common with aesthetic appreciations. (This point may be contested on the grounds that there is in fact an 'ethics of belief', a moral value in getting at the truth. Discussion of this would require a further treatment than is possible here.) The real relevance of 'worthwhileness' to morality here is that no subject would be regarded as worthwhile in the educational sense if it is immoral; but subjects may well be worth learning even though they have no 'moral' dimension. Subjects have to pass a negative test as regards morality, not a positive one.

Another approach to the conclusion that morality is a necessary part of education is this: it has been maintained, as was indicated in chapter 3, that there are a number of distinct 'forms' of knowledge and understanding which men have evolved, different ways of looking at the world, all of which are essential to an adequate, or rational, comprehension of the human condition. Mathematics is one of these forms, science is another, aesthetics another, and so on. Initiation into these distinct forms of experience is needed to make a rational mind. It is claimed that morals, like religion, is one of these ways of understanding the human situation, and that without an entry into these specific areas a man lacks the basis for rationality of this particular kind. If this is so, then education, which is a means of initiating the young into these various forms of knowledge, must necessarily involve initiation into morals. For unless it does so the pupil is not properly equipped to act as a rational creature in that important area. A similar argument could be used to justify the inclusion of each and every one of the different forms; that failing any of them the pupil would not be 'educated'. At this point we may remark that the argument depends upon a stipulative or definitional meaning being given to the term 'education'. If 'education' is understood as initiation into a number of different but essential forms of knowledge, and morals are accepted as one of those essential forms, then it follows of necessity that the teaching of morals must be a part of education, and education must be a 'moral' concern. This, however, is simply a matter of stipulation. We could always deny that someone who had not undergone some moral instruction was 'properly educated' since, given the stipulation, 'properly educated' means, amongst other things, having had some moral training. But to talk of being 'properly educated' in this all-or-nothing way is to take up a position which does not altogether conform with popular usage. It doesn't seem absurd or self-contradictory to say of someone that he is well educated but totally lacking in moral understanding. We would presumably have to say of such a man that he was educated but that there were areas of understanding in which he was deficient, morals for one. We should have to say something of the same sort about one who, though otherwise educated, knew nothing about science, or art, or medicine, or law. Education is not a matter of all or nothing and we do not withhold the term 'educated' from those who are uninformed in one or two areas, however important these areas may be. Thus it would probably be more true to say that moral instruction is a desirable part of a general education, although only contingently so. Another way of putting this is to say that moral education is not a necessary part of education in the sense that every teacher is or must be a teacher of morals. When a teacher is teaching mathematics or history or science he is not, or at least he need not be, engaged in moral teaching. These subjects, although value-loaded, are not 'morally loaded'. They are neutral in respect of morals. Moral education is a distinct kind of education, like mathematical education. Moral education is thus a constituent part of the enterprise of education, and necessary in the practical sense that without it education is not complete. But it is not necessarily involved in education in the way in which the requirement that what is taught should be worth learning is necessarily involved in it. In other words, a 'moral' content is not part of the definition of the term 'education'. To make it so would simply be to restrict the term in a way that does not accord with our ordinary understanding of it. The teacher is, of course, in his role as educator bound to practise morality in his teaching. He is bound to use morally acceptable procedures and to show respect for his pupils as persons. But to teach in a morally acceptable manner is not, as such, the same thing as engaging in moral education.

### 3 Moral education

Given that morality is an important though not logically necessary part of a general education, the question now to be answered is: what is involved in moral education? Plainly it is, to begin with, a matter of transmitting knowledge. Moral education has to do with influencing behaviour and this presupposes a certain amount of knowledge to be acquired by the pupil. Children are not born moral: they have to be made so, and an indispensable part of this enterprise is that of equipping them with a certain conceptual apparatus. It is plain that a child will not be able to choose to do the right thing unless he knows what it is. He will not be able to attach any sense to the teaching that he ought to keep a promise if he doesn't know what a promise is, and it is useless to tell a child that he ought not to steal if he doesn't know the meaning of 'steal', and so on. Moral knowledge is thus an indispensable part of moral education. This acquisition of knowledge will involve an understanding of moral concepts like 'right', 'wrong', 'duty' and 'promise' together with a grasp of rules like 'One ought to tell the truth, to keep a promise, to pay debts, to be kind to others.' How a child is given this knowledge and understanding is a matter of moral pedagogy. Two main tasks come under this heading. Firstly, the child must be initiated into 'moral' language; he must be taught to handle the concepts and he must learn the rules. Secondly, he must be encouraged to act according to the rules. He must be encouraged to speak the truth, keep his promises and be considerate to others. This latter aspect of the task is moral training, which consists in getting children to act in morally acceptable ways, to abide by the moral code of their society. This is an elementary form of morality: acting in accordance with customary social expectations.

The teacher's task in moral training has been facilitated during the past twenty or thirty years by detailed studies, carried out by child psychologists and others, concerning the way in which a child's moral consciousness develops. These studies, of which Piaget's and Kohlberg's are important examples, do not belong to the field of moral philosophy or of philosophy of education, but they enter into educational theory by providing information about the way in which children develop and so enable teachers to engage in moral training more effectively than might otherwise be possible. The findings referred to are detailed and complicated and will not be gone into here. The general conclusions differ between one theorist and another, but they amount to this: that, as is the case with a child's intellectual life, his moral consciousness develops in stages. [18] There is an initial stage of non-morality, in which the child is not really conscious of rules or obligations. Then comes a stage in which rules are recognised and generally obeyed, but are regarded as arbitrary and as imposed from without, obedience being given simply as a matter of prudence. A further stage is where rules are accepted as fixed and unalterable but dependent upon some sort of group approval or authority. Then, finally, the child comes to see the point of the rules, as limitations which make social life possible, and comes eventually to 'internalise' them, adopting them for his own. This progression, from a non-moral position to one of recognition and appreciation, from heteronomy to moral autonomy, is seen as a logically invariant sequence. For Piaget it depends to some extent on maturation; for Kohlberg it is the consequence of the interaction of the child with social forces and institutions. The pedagogical implications are that, although little can be done in school about the actual stages of development, since these are a matter of maturation or of social interaction, what can be done is to provide moral teaching which fits in with the stage of development the child has at any given time reached. Moral training is thus parallel to intellectual training. There are points of 'readiness' in the moral life as there are in the intellectual life, and the moral educator must be aware of them and ready to organise his teaching accordingly.

So far we have been dealing with one aspect of moral teaching; moral training, which is simply a matter of getting the child to keep, out of habit, the rules of his society. The previous paragraph, however, indicates a further step to be taken. For we do not want the child merely to keep the rules as such. We want him to be something more than morally trained: we want him to be morally educated. This means bringing him to a position of moral autonomy, in which the rules are *his* rules, rules he keeps because he recognises them as rules he ought to keep quite apart from any considerations of prudence, praise or blame. This means giving him a rationale for the rules, a reason why. The morally educated person is one who not only knows what he ought to do, but knows also the reason why he ought to do it. This supplying of a rationale is by no means a simple affair, and it is here that the moral educator may look to moral philosophy for help. The moral philosopher, it will be remembered, is not concerned with offering moral advice, or with making moral theories, but with a clarification of the concepts used in moral discourse and with the scrutiny of the arguments used in moral theories. What he can do by way of help to the moral educator is to set out a schema within which a rationale may be given. This may best be done by setting out the structure of a moral argument. A moral argument is a kind of syllogism in reverse, an argument from a particular case to a general practical principle. Suppose, for example, a teacher makes a moral judgment, that a certain action is wrong, that a child has told a lie and ought not to have done so. Suppose now that the culprit asks: why not? The teacher has to give a reason, a rationale for his judgment. He says: because we have a moral rule: no one should tell lies. In many cases, no doubt, this appeal to a rule would be enough to satisfy the questioner. Suppose, however, that the child questions the rule: why do we have such a rule? The rule now needs to be justified. This will involve an appeal to a higher-order rule, a moral principle. This might be, for example: everyone ought to behave so as to maintain a general feeling of trust and security, and telling lies threatens this feeling of mutual trust. Once again, this reason may be sufficient. If, however, the questioner challenges the principle, a further reason must be given, this time an appeal to a more fundamental principle still. This might be: everyone ought to act so as to promote as much human well-being as possible. Telling lies, by threatening the general sense of trust in society, threatens this general well-being, therefore one should not tell lies. And it follows from this that the particular lie in question should not have been told.

Of course, the way in which this would be explained to a child would depend upon his age and comprehension, but this form of argument underlies all moral education, as distinct from moral training. What has been exemplified here is the giving of a rationale at different levels of generality, and the justification of the original judgment has been carried upwards to the point where no further reasons can be given. No further moral reason can be adduced to support a fundamental moral principle. It is not suggested here that the fundamental principle used in the example above is the only one which might be used. It is the principle which sustains the moral theory known as Utilitarianism, which makes the ultimate moral rationale the extent to which actions conduce towards human happiness or well-being.[20] There are other fundamental principles which might have been used, deriving from other moral theories. The important point is, however, that the rationale eventually involves some fundamental principle which is the basis of the whole argument. Moral education requires that the pupil should, at last, accept rules and principles and make them his own.

We should guard against a possible misconception here. Moral training has been distinguished from moral education in that the first involves getting the pupil to do what he ought to do whilst the second involves the giving of an adequate rationale for what is required as a moral duty and of getting the pupil to accept the rationale as adequate. It is not suggested that moral training comes first and then, at some later time, moral education begins. The two processes go on together. It is important that children should be morally trained, that they should be got to do the right thing out of habit. This requires a regime of precepts and practices, in which parents and teachers impose certain standards of conduct on children. Children have to learn what to do, and be got to do it, by pressures of one kind or another. But concurrently with this they may be given explanations, suitable to their ability to appreciate them, according, that is, to the stage of moral development they have reached. Such explanations would need to be relatively unsophisticated to begin with, but as the child grows older and becomes more aware of the human and social issues involved, the rationale can be given in more adult and sophisticated terms.

What has been maintained in this section is this: to be morally educated the pupil must, firstly, acquire moral knowledge, knowledge about what he ought to do and what not to do. Secondly, he must acquire knowledge of a justificatory kind. He must know *why* he ought to behave in some ways and not in others; he must be in possession of an adequate rationale. Thirdly, he must be disposed to act, and generally act, in moral ways out of a conviction that it is right to do so. He must act from a moral motive. To meet all these requirements is to be morally mature. It is necessary to make this last qualification because moral education, like education in general, is not a matter of all or nothing. It is possible for a person to be morally educated in the sense that he has moral knowledge, and yet consistently fail to act according to that knowledge. It is difficult to know what exactly to say of such a person. We could call him morally educated but weak, or imperfectly educated morally, but it would be difficult to deny that he was, in some sense, or to some degree, morally educated. We could perhaps meet the difficulty by saying that his mentors had failed him on the training side, since they had failed to ensure that he habitually did what he knew he ought to do.

## 4 Moral education and teaching

Although morality involves knowledge and practice it is not one of the traditional timetable subjects and its place in the school curriculum is somewhat imprecise. The point was made earlier that morality was not a necessary part of education in the sense of being necessarily involved in all other subjects, but that it was, rather, a special sort of education, an important constituent of a general education, like mathematics and science. Such a view should, logically, involve the admission of 'morality' as a separate discipline, alongside the others. This, however, would run counter to contemporary practice in this country where, as a matter of fact, 'moral education', in so far as it is given, tends to be interwoven with other subjects, some of which are more effective vehicles for this purpose than others. Because of the close connection between religion and morals, moral education is perhaps more easily undertaken in lessons devoted to religious studies than in, say geography or mathematics classes; and lessons in literature and history may provide more opportunities for moral instruction than lessons in art and craft or economics. However, the comparative ease with which some subjects may deal with moral issues raises some possible difficulties. It could be argued that it is not really the business of history teaching or the teaching of literature to get involved in lower-order moral considerations. It is the pupil's task to understand what went on in history, to study the interplay of historical causes and effects, not to learn how to moralise about it or to draw moral lessons from it. It is the teacher's job to see that the pupil gets some historical understanding, not to use history as an opportunity for moralising. The same might be said about the study of literature. Aesop, La Fontaine and Jane Austen were all moralists, and if we wanted to teach moral lessons as such, these writers would provide plenty of illuminating examples for study. But if Aesop, La Fontaine, Shakespeare, Milton and Jane Austen are studied as contributors to literature, then the morality embodied in their writings should be the subject of knowledge and understanding, as part of the subject matter, not as material for moral persuasion. This is, no doubt, a contentious point, and more needs to be said on it. It may be that there is inevitably a carry-over between history and morality and between

103

literature and morality, but it would be wrong to see these subjects as peculiarly 'moral' subjects in the way that, say, trigonometry and chemistry are not. It is more important that pupils should *understand* the characters, motives, and policies of Henry VIII and Napoleon, Iago and Macbeth, than that they should learn to moralise about them or hear someone else do so. If morality is to be taught as a distinct form of knowledge it should be taught as such, drawing on such historical and literary material as may be appropriate; but its proper place in the curriculum lies outside the history or the literature lesson.

If there is anything in this contention, and bearing in mind the general reluctance in this country to timetable lessons in morality, then it might plausibly be argued that moral education in schools is best conducted quite informally, seizing opportunities and occasions as they arise for the inculcation of moral truths and recommendations. Children have to acquire the rules and the principles and become aware of the rationales which may be offered, but this can perhaps be best done on an ad hoc basis. Children may be made more sensitive to the needs and feelings of others in a variety of ways in the daily come-and-go of the classroom; dealing with pets, with other children, with children who are handicapped or disadvantaged in some way, and so far as older children are concerned, by helping others outside the school, elderly or sick people for example. A general form teacher will usually have plenty of opportunities brought up in class discussions on issues like vandalism, sexual behaviour, race relations and the like to enable him to make moral points and to link them up to the moral principles involved. It is probably in this way that the approach to moral autonomy by the child may be most effectively encouraged.

It will have been noticed that in the paragraph above the discussion has strayed from what is strictly philosophy of education to what is more properly a limited theory of education, a theory about the way moral education may best be brought about. This progression seems natural in the context, but it serves as an example of the point made in chapter 1 that the distinction made there between philosophy of education and educational theory tends on occasion to be blurred at the edges.

## 5 Religion and education

It is appropriate to include a brief section on religion and education here since religion and morals have been traditionally very closely connected. What the actual connection between them amounts to is open to argument, but it is a fact that those who are committed to a religious position almost invariably hold pronounced views on morality. The connection between religion and education has also been a very close one in most cases, and the claim that religion must have an important place in education has always had, in this country at any rate, influential support.

The connection between religion and morality may be considered first. This topic is not strictly central to philosophy of education but belongs rather to the philosophy of religion, or perhaps to moral philosophy proper. Many educationalists, however, although by no means all, will accept the claims of both religion and morals as candidates for inclusion in an educational syllabus. But since the claim is sometimes made that religious teaching is indispensable to education on the grounds that education is a moral matter and that without religion there can be no morality, the connection between religion and morality must be examined here, however inadequately. This supposed connection may be, in philosophical terms, either necessary or contingent. Religion and morality may be held to be connected in such a way that unless one is committed to a religious point of view one cannot be a truly moral person. It is difficult to believe that any responsible person seriously holds this view nowadays. It is belied by the undoubted existence of agnostics and atheists who nonetheless live moral lives, and the position can only be maintained by the implausible suggestion that such people are 'really' religious in spite of their avowed denials. A philosophical rebuttal of this 'necessary connection' view centres on any attempt to equate concepts like 'morally good' with 'according to God's will or purposes'. If such an equation were accepted then it would necessarily follow that there can be no morality which does not have a religious force. But any such attempt to maintain the strict connection by an equivalence or definition is self-defeating. It prevents, for example, anyone from making a substantial, informative statement to the effect that God's will and God's purposes are morally good. This is because, granted the equation, all that the assertion succeeds in saying is that God's will is according to God's will, or that God's purposes are according to God's purposes, both of which may be true but are certainly tautological, giving no real information at all. The same difficulty arises from any attempt to equate 'morally good' with 'what God approves of'. The fact that God approves of an action and the fact that it is a morally good action are two separate facts, if facts they are. The morality of an action doesn't depend upon, nor is it the same as, God's approval of it. In order to praise God's will and God's purposes as being morally good we should need to have an independent criterion of 'morally good' and then register the fact that God's will and purposes squared with it. There is no necessary connection between what God wills and what is morally good although it may be true that God only wills what is morally good.

This all amounts to saying that religion and morals are connected only contingently. It is a matter of fact that practically every religion has a code of morals built into it, but it is doubtful whether this is anything more than a matter of fact. It doesn't seem self-contradictory to suppose that there could be a religion which imposed only prudential obligations on its adherents. The fact that no major religion is like this is quite empirical and contingent. It is certainly true that not all moral codes require a religious sanction or depend upon religious beliefs. It is possible to maintain a strictly moral position whilst denying or reserving judgment on the religious issue. Religion may, and almost invariably does, provide a powerful sanction for moral action when the agent subscribes to the religious belief, but this sanction and the beliefs which go with it are not *necessary* to morality, either in the philosophical or the practical sense.

The connection between religion and education may be dealt with in much the same way as the connection between morality and education. An extreme view would be to regard education simply as a device for serving a religious purpose. Froebel tended to such a view. For him the education of a child was a matter of bringing out a divine pattern implicit in the child.[5] Cardinal Newman, whilst perhaps not saying so explicitly, obviously regarded education as serving the same overall purpose as the church to which he belonged. [14] Thus, to initiate a pupil into mathematics, science and history is to bring him into contact with the Divine Purpose as revealed in the world. Education is, as it were, religious in essence. Its subject matter is the Divine Order and Providence, as revealed in various ways. Religion then would be necessarily a part of education, or perhaps it would be more true to say that education is an essential part of religion. There are objections to this somewhat strong view of the matter. For one thing, it tends to beg an important question, assuming for the purposes of argument the truth of conclusions about the existence of God and the nature of his purposes, conclusions which not everyone would want to accept. Secondly, to establish a necessary connection between religion and education by means of a definition or stipulation is an easy but empty move. It is simply to deny, by a verbalism, the possibility of a purely secular education, a denial which would leave the reality unchanged.

An alternative view is that religion may be held to be essential or necessary to education in that the religious dimension constitutes one of the forms of knowledge by means of which men come to make sense of their world and their experience. Religion would thus take its place with science and mathematics and art as one way of structuring human experience, and is necessary in that without it some significant aspects of experience would be left uncared for. So religious education would be a special sort of education, like moral education, aesthetic education and mathematical education. There is much to be said for such a view. It is true that without some sort of religious education a great deal of what goes on in our contemporary life would be puzzling if not quite incomprehensible. Our society is informed with the ideas and traditions of Christianity, and it is difficult to see what a child could make of much of our way of life, many sayings, allusions, proverbs, social institutions, the churches, the great cathedrals, much of our greatest music, painting and poetry, if he had not been initiated into the tradition to which they all belong. As was said in an earlier chapter, all these are part of our heritage and not to introduce a child to them and to the religious tradition that sustains them is to deny him membership of his estate. But, as was suggested when dealing with the claim of morals to be a necessary part of education, the 'necessary' inclusion of religion, even in the limited sense of teaching children about the tradition, depends upon a stipulative account of education. If to be educated involves initiation into all the forms of knowledge, then if religion is one of those forms, 'education' requires its inclusion as a matter of necessity. Education, however, is not a matter of all or nothing, and those who are not initiated into religious knowledge, in the sense of information about religion, need not, as such, be denied the epithet 'educated'. At worst they could be said to be incompletely educated.

## 6 Religious education and teaching

Supposing, as we may, that religious education is a special kind of education which may take its place in the curriculum with other such kinds, a major problem needs to be raised concerning it. Religious education or religious studies may be approached in two markedly different ways: the way of understanding and the way of commitment. Granted the case for the inclusion of religion in the curriculum there can be no serious objection to the approach which aims at the giving of information and the improvement of understanding. Education requires this. This approach takes religion and its works as empirical matters and seeks to give an understanding of how they came to be as they are. Religious studies would have historical and social elements built into them, as well as material from anthropology and mythology. There is no reason why such studies should be confined to the Christian religion. In a multi-cultural society there is a good case for some form of comparative religious studies, both on intellectual and social grounds. The way of commitment raises more difficult considerations. For this would involve teaching children not only *about* religion, but also trying to get them seriously to adopt some religious point of view, to make them committed or practising Christians, Moslems or Sikhs. The acceptability of this as an educational strategy turns on the view one takes of religious knowledge or belief. In so far as what is taught is *about* religion, about its origins and development, its forms, rituals, beliefs and practices, it is accountable to evidence. What is taught may be shown to be accurate or not. But the knowledge on which religious commitment must be grounded is not of this kind. It is in fact religious doctrine, and about this it is not usually the case that evidence will settle the question of its truth or falsity. One of the objections to including religion amongst the 'forms of knowledge' is that whilst other forms may plausibly be said to have 'tests for truth' there is little, if any, general agreement about what constitutes a test for truth in religion. This means that religious education aimed at securing commitment runs very close to indoctrination, the teaching of uncheckable propositions by authority.

It would be possible and indeed useful to take up an intermediate position between the view of religious education which sees it simply as giving knowledge about religion and the view which requires it to give a sense of commitment. The teacher could try to develop in the child a religious consciousness, by getting him to understand how life looked to, say, the Hebrew prophets, to Jesus, to St Francis, to Buddha or to Mohammed. This would help to provide perspectives on the world which would be necessary before anyone could really be in a position to choose to commit himself, or not, to any particular religion.

In making a distinction between knowledge of empirical fact and a commitment to doctrine we are faced with a problem which arose also in the assessment of a moral education. What could properly be said of someone who had a detailed knowledge of religion as a human, historical and institutional reality but who was in no way committed to any religious doctrine or belief? It would seem equally wrong to assert or to deny that he was educated in respect of religion. We would probably have to say that he knew a lot about religion

111

but was not a religious man, as we might say of another that he had a great deal of moral understanding but was not a moral man. The religious education of the first had left him short of being religious, whilst the moral education of the other had left him short of being a moral man. We may note, however, that whilst the latter judgment would involve a degree of condemnation, it is not so clearly the case with the former.

## 7 Conclusion

This chapter set out to deal with two complicated topics, the relationship which exists between morals and religion, and that which holds between these two areas and education. It is concerned, that is to say, with the meaning of moral and religious education, and with the justification of morality and religion as candidates for inclusion in the curriculum. It is hardly to be expected that its conclusions would be uncomplicated or uncontentious. It has been suggested that neither morals nor religion should be held as monopolising the educational enterprise and that neither should be regarded as permeating every aspect of education. Moral education and religious education, it is argued, are specific forms of education, both necessary in their way to a complete education, but neither necessary in the sense of being the whole point and purpose of education. Moral education, it is argued, involves giving children knowledge about what to do in respect of behaviour which affects the well-being of others, together with an understanding of the rationale involved. Since moral education is closely linked with moral training, a person who was fully educated, morally, would be one who not only knew what he ought to do and why he ought to do it, but was also disposed to act consistently in the light of this knowledge. Religious education, similarly, involves the acquisition of knowledge, knowledge about religion certainly, but whether a complete religious education would imply commitment to a belief in the truth of religious doctrines is a matter for controversy.

## Suggestions for further reading

There is no end to the books about morals and moral philosophy but many of them are technical and difficult for beginners. A very clear introduction to the classical theories of morals is given in R.S. Peters, *Ethics and Education*, chapter 3. This book gives a thorough and detailed working out of the moral basis of education and is essential reading for any student of the philosophy of education.

A fairly comprehensive treatment of the contemporary study of moral philosophy is by W.D. Hudson, *Modern Moral Philosophy* (Macmillan, 1970). This book is not specifically directed towards education, however, and may be found demanding by newcomers to the subject. It is, nonetheless, clear, sound and readable.

An outline of the developmental approach to moral education is R.S. Peters, 'The Place of Kohlberg's Theory in Moral Education', in *Essays on Educators*.

The place of religion and religious education in schools is a highly contentious topic and although there has been a good deal written on it much of what has been written is not strictly philosophical in treatment. The subject is dealt with by P.H. Hirst in *Knowledge and the Curriculum*, chapter 12, and by R. Marples in

'Is Religious Education Possible?' in the *Journal of the Philosophy of Education Society of Great Britain*, vol. 12, 1978.

# Social philosophy of education 6

## 1 Introduction

Previous chapters in this book have stressed the fact that education has close links with other important aspects of human life, with human nature, with the growth and development of children, with knowledge and understanding, with morals and religion. Another obviously close connection is that between education and the ordering of human society. Education may be seen as one of the devices which society employs to preserve its present integrity and its future survival. In its descriptive sense 'education' is simply the name of a complicated network of institutions and practices designed to bring the young into society by initiating them into the current culture, the intricate pattern of practices, assumptions and expectations which make up social life. Thus education and its practices will form part the subject – matter of various social sciences. The sociologist of education, the student of comparative education and the historian of education all try to deal with education as a social phenomenon, and their work results in social theories *about* education. In *The Republic* Plato was, among other things, giving a social theory about the role of education. Education for him was a means of providing the elites needed to govern the ideal state. [19] For the sociologist Durkheim, education was a means of integrating and consolidating the bonds which ensured a stable society. [4] For Dewey, education was a device to facilitate what was for him the most desirable kind of society, a democracy. [2] In each case a social theory was being offered, and from one point of view the theories mentioned can be regarded as descriptive in character, setting out what it is assumed education can, or does, do in society. An important question to ask in each case would be whether the theory offered was, factually, an adequate one: whether or not education can do or does do what is claimed for it. To the extent to which educational theories are of this kind they are descriptive sociological theories, and in so far as the philosopher of education is concerned with them it would be with the conceptual apparatus employed and with the consistency of the arguments used. The theories themselves would be validated by, and be subject to, empirical evidence.

There are, however, social theories of education with which the philosopher is more centrally concerned, those which are prescriptive in character, which argue that education *ought* to serve certain social ends whether in fact it does so or not. Such theories are ideological theories. The theories of Plato, Durkheim and Dewey mentioned above have, besides a descriptive function, a prescriptive function. Plato thinks that education *ought* to bring about the kind of society outlined in *The Republic*; Durkheim, that education ought to aim at a stable and cohesive society; and Dewey, that the desirable outcome of education would be a democratic and cooperative way of life. Prescriptive, or ideological, theories of education enter largely into present-day thinking about education. It is often argued, for example, that education should aim at producing a society of equals, that there should be 'equality' in education, or 'equality of opportunity'. Again, it is argued that education is a means to freedom and that there ought to be 'education for freedom' or 'freedom in education'. There is a continuing argument for democracy in education, that education ought to be directed towards the establishment or presentation of a democratic way of life, and that to this end education ought to be 'democratic' in character. This consideration of what education ought to be is quite distinct from the consideration of what education actually does do, although social theorists, like Durkheim and Dewey, do not always clearly distinguish between them. These prescriptive social theories of education are really general theories of an ideological kind and the philosopher of education is concerned with their credentials and acceptability. In this concluding chapter three social theories of education will be examined briefly: the theory that education should be concerned with equality, that education should be about freedom, and that education should serve the cause of democracy. A detailed working out of these ideological theories and an examination of all the assumptions involved in them would be well beyond the scope of this book. This chapter will deal only with the root idea contained in each: the ideas of equality, freedom and democracy, in so far as they are relevant to and may be justified in educational practice.

## 2 Equality and education

One great difficulty in dealing with equality as a theory

is its exasperating vagueness. The term is often used in political slogans of the 'all men are equal' kind, but it is rarely made very clear what is meant in saying this. It is perhaps best to begin by recognising that a, perhaps the, basic meaning of 'equal' is 'the same' or 'the same in some specified sense'. Two lines of equal length are lines of the same length, two men of equal height are the same height, and so on. This is a straightforward and relatively uncomplicated meaning, the meaning usually understood outside of a political or philosophical discussion. Now, if this is what 'equal' means, the slogan 'all men are equal' is in most cases false, since men are not in any interesting sense the same. Of course, it is more than probable that the egalitarian who asserts that all men are equal is not trying to say that all men are the same. He may say that the purport of the slogan is not that men are the same descriptively, but that they ought to be treated the same, in the same way. This avoids the empirical error but runs into other difficulties. For if anyone seriously asserts that everyone ought to be treated the same, or alike, it is sufficient to point out that to do so would run counter to certain other practical principles most people hold. We do not think, for example, that innocent men should be treated as we treat criminals, that sick people should be treated as we treat healthy people, that children should be fed and clothed as we think adults should be. Treating all alike would offend against our notions of appropriateness. People have different needs and we recognise that this should be borne in mind. It would also offend against our notions of fairness. People have different needs, but they also have different deserts, and these too, we think, should be recognised and provided for. A strict

118

egalitarian principle would, presumably, require that men should be treated alike, notwithstanding their different needs and deserts. Of course the egalitarian, faced with the logic of his position, would be very likely to declare, once more, that this wasn't what he meant at all, and charity would require us to accept his disclaimer. He might then put forward a view more acceptable to our moral and commonsense notions, that is, that men should be treated the same only when their needs and their deserts are the same, and that when they have different needs or different deserts, they should be dealt with differently. But this principle, which hardly anyone would want to contest, is not the principle of equality; it is the principle of justice. Aristotle made the point clearly enough when he declared that justice demands that we treat like cases alike and unlike cases differently. It is our almost instinctive adherence to the principle of justice that gives interest to the biblical parable of the labourers in the vineyard, where those who came late in the day received the same wages as those who had worked since daybreak. We have a feeling that this was somehow wrong, or unfair, and the interest of the story lies in the resolution of this seeming injustice. Let us notice, here, however, that we have shifted our attention from 'equality' to 'justice', which are plainly not the same thing and need not coincide in practice. They coincide only when deserts or needs are the same in the cases under consideration. Then, and only then, is it just to treat people equally or 'the same'. Otherwise, to treat different situations in the same way would usually be inappropriate and often unjust. Fair treatment, just treatment, involves taking account of differences in people's circumstances, and this will often mean treating them differently. Equality as such has no great virtue. Equal treatment, in any substantial sense, is morally and practically acceptable only when it accords with our sense of justice, and the only sense in which all men, without exception, should be treated the same is that they should be treated justly.

The educational implications of this analysis are considerable. If we take the 'equality' principle in its strict sense, in that all children are the same, or that they should all be treated alike in any substantial sense, the absurdity of the suggestion is obvious. For children are not the same in any significant educational sense, and, leaving deserts aside, are not the same in respect of their educational needs. To treat all alike, the intelligent and the less so, the well adjusted, the emotionally disturbed, would be grossly inappropriate and no one would advocate this. Yet this is what the principle, strictly understood, requires. If the egalitarian does not mean this then he must abandon the principle of equality thus understood. For what is really required is not equal treatment but fair treatment, appropriate treatment, a fair consideration of children's different needs and requirements, in other words educational justice. This would be consistent with, indeed imply, the provision of special classes, perhaps special schools, both for the gifted and the less able, with all the institutional paraphernalia of grades, testing, selection, streaming and setting which causes such concern to the egalitarian in education. Now, in practice hardly anyone is likely to deny the proposition that children should be treated according to their different educational needs, so that an insistence on strict equality in education would be simply a form of crankiness. It is then pertinent to ask just what substance there could be in the theory that there ought to be such equality. Is the egalitarian simply asking that educational resources should be distributed fairly? If so, then one can agree with him but ask why the point should be put in terms of equality rather than that of fairness.

At this point the egalitarian might retort that he is not so much concerned with abstract 'equality', as with something else, namely 'equality of opportunity', and go on to claim that all children should be granted equal opportunity in education. But, given a strict interpretation of 'equality' this move raises difficulties of its own. For the opportunities in question may be those of access to educational goods like schools and teachers, or those of achievement in education, educational outcome. In neither case is strict equality possible nor is it always desirable. Children cannot, as a matter of fact, be given the same access to educational goods since these goods themselves differ in quality. There are good schools and good teachers and there are less good schools and less efficient teachers. It might be possible to make all schools open to all comers, irrespective of needs and other considerations, but since the schools are variable in quality this would not give equal access in the substantial sense of the 'same' access. Nor would it be altogether desirable, since not all schools would be suitable for all pupils. What is required is that children should go to those schools which best meet their needs and abilities, and that no child should be kept out of a suitable school on non-educational grounds, because his parents are poor, for example, or because he is of a certain religious or racial group. A policy like this would be fair and humane, and so highly desirable, but it

121

would not be giving equal opportunities so far as access to education is concerned. 'Equal access' would justify admitting a tone-deaf child into a cathedral choir school; simple humanity and a sense of appropriateness would recognise this as absurd. Nor is equality of opportunity for achievement in education possible in practice. It is not possible because children differ in their abilities and expectations. Nor would it be in practice desirable. The only way to achieve an equal outcome between one child and another would be to fix the norm of achievement low enough to allow everyone to meet it and then to make sure that those who could better it were not allowed to do so. Merely to state this is to show it to be quite unacceptable as a practical educational programme.

Equality in education, then, will not do as a theory. At best it is a muddled way of calling for justice. Justice in education, however, involves differential treatment for pupils, to suit their different requirements, and the organisation and provision of education is to be judged, not by the extent to which it promotes equality or equal opportunity, but by the extent to which it deals with children fairly in what it has to offer them. In so far as this claim for equality in education is part of a general theory of education, the same conclusion holds. An 'equal' society of 'equal' men would not meet our common standards of morality and appropriateness, a just society would.

## 3 Freedom and education

Freedom, like equality, is one of those concepts not only complicated in themselves but which carry with them a strong emotive force which disposes people in their favour and makes a critical examination of them more than usually difficult. What follows is, inevitably, a somewhat simplistic view, but one which tries to bring out the main issues so far as they are relevant to education.

The basic idea involved in 'freedom' is that of not being impeded, of being let alone to do what one wants to do. There is a long-standing tradition in political and social philosophy which sees freedom as the situation in which a man is not hindered or constrained by others. [8 chapter 21] I am free when no one is actively preventing me from doing what I have a mind to do. Others may hinder me or prevent me either by using actual physical force or by passing laws which are indirect ways of exercising force. Outside of this exercise of force I am free. A complicating factor which may be dealt with briefly here is that a man may be hindered by circumstances which do not amount to restraint by others, that is, by his own shortcomings, physical, mental, financial and social. There is for example, a sense in which I am quite free to buy an estate in the Bahamas and to play Beethoven's *Violin Concerto*. Neither of these activities are forbidden to me, by force or by law. Yet I am unable to do either since I have not enough money for the first nor the technical skill required for the second. In other words I may be free to do something but unable to do it. Poverty, ignorance and lack of ability are not really obstacles to freedom, although they are often spoken of as though they were. On the other hand I may be able to do things which I am not free to do. I may be able to make a political speech although, if the authorities forbid, I will not be free to make it. This distinction between freedom and ability has considerable social implications, and is certainly relevant to education. A child is, so to say, free to read the whole corpus of French literature, in that no one is likely to prevent him from doing so; but if he is unable to read French or to read at all, he will be unable to do what he is certainly free to do. This is an important point. It is sometimes said that education increases an individual's freedom, giving him freedom to do what otherwise he could not do. This seems to be incorrect. Education does not increase freedom except in those special cases where an educational qualification is needed to comply with a law or regulation, where the law will be invoked against anyone who is not so qualified. What, in general, education can do is to increase one's ability, to enable one to make use of the freedom one already has. Everyone in this country is free to read Shakespeare, to appreciate the music of Mozart, to write, to exchange ideas with others; no law or force will prevent them. But these activities presuppose and entail knowledge, skills, and abilities of various kinds. Education is a means of acquiring the abilities without which this freedom is not worth very much. The freedom, however, does not depend on, or arise out of the education. Freedom rests on laws, regulations, social decisions. Freedom, in so far as it is a good, is a political good. Education may enable people to make use of a good made possible by the social system in which they live.

So far we have spoken of 'freedom' and it was suggested that this concept carries strong emotive overtones. Freedom is generally regarded as a good, something worth having. Yet, if pressed, most people would allow that perhaps freedom is not altogether a good thing. Freedom may be abused. It is possible to have too much freedom. Children, it may be said, can have more freedom than is good for them. It is as well to recognise this and to admit that freedom may sometimes be overvalued, that not all freedom is good. One way of dealing with this ambivalence about freedom is to avoid using the general term 'freedom' as far as possible and to talk instead of 'freedoms'. We have an indefinite number of possible freedoms, possibilities of not being hindered or prevented by others. Some of these possible freedoms we rate very highly: the freedom to live where we please, to marry whom we please, to choose our own friends, to choose our rulers. Some possible freedoms we do not rate highly at all and would want to discourage: the freedoms to steal, to rape, to defraud others. These many possible freedoms may be ordered in a hierarchy, with the more important freedoms towards the top, the ones we disapprove of towards the bottom. The function of the law and public opinion is to draw the line between those possible freedoms we want to encourage and those we want to put an end to. Thus, the law extinguishes some possible freedoms to give effect to other, more desirable ones. The distinction between desirable and undesirable freedoms rests on the extent to which we see that some freedoms produce good results, happiness and justice for example, whilst others are likely to bring about harm, or more harm than good.

This analysis may be applied to freedoms in an educational context. It has been suggested that education does not give freedom or increase it but simply allows individuals to make use of the freedoms they have already. It will now be maintained that the practice

125

of education presupposes certain freedoms, both for the pupil and for the teacher. The pupil must be free to attend school. He must be free to participate in what goes on there: he must be free to make use of the facilities available to him there. Likewise, the teacher must have the freedoms necessary for him to carry out his task. He must be free to organise his work, to adapt his methods to the requirements of his pupils, to exercise authority over them. Without these freedoms education could hardly be carried on at all. The interesting question, however, is just where to draw the line between those freedoms which are permissible and necessary and those which are not.

There are some freedoms for his pupils that the teacher will feel bound to discourage: the freedom to be dishonest, or disorderly, or inattentive; since if these freedoms are allowed, his effectiveness as a teacher will be reduced and education to that extent frustrated. There are other possible freedoms which he may or may not be prepared to allow: the freedom to move about the room, to work with other children, to choose one's own work or one's own ways of working. The matter becomes problematic when it is recognised that the criteria upon which such freedoms are allowed or forbidden may themselves be variable. Throughout this book a distinction has been made between two very general theories of education, between the view which sees education as a transaction between an authority and a subordinate, and the view which regards it as an enterprise involving the growth and development of an individual as a result of his interaction with and participation in an educational environment, the distinction between the traditional and progressivist outlooks.

126

On the whole it may be expected that the traditionalist will be prepared to countenance fewer classroom freedoms than will the committed progressivist. The traditionalist, taking his stand on the prime importance of knowledge and discipline, will tend to emphasise a rigidity of structure in the business of teaching and learning. Children will be expected to be quiet, attentive, teacher-directed, and when they are allowed to exercise initiative it will usually be within a teacher-organised context. The progressivist, with an eye on the personal development of his pupils, will be inclined to emphasise the need for spontaneous activity, self-imposed discipline and individual discovery, and so be fairly tolerant of freedoms within the classroom, regarding them as the necessary conditions of spontaneity. Carried to extremes, we have, on the one hand, the disciplinarian who reduces pupil freedom to a minimum on the assumption that any relaxation of discipline will lead to chaos and the end of education, on the other, the idealistic progressivist who regards any imposition by adults on the child's spontaneity of impulse and freedom as tantamount to indoctrination and so immoral. These are, of course, extremes. The truth which underlies each of these approaches is that the degree of freedom justified in the classroom will depend on the extent to which such freedom serves the end of education. If granting a freedom results in improved pupil performance, it would be foolish not to grant it; if a given freedom leads to noise, disruption, indiscipline, indifferent or shoddy work, then this would be a good reason for discouraging it. Freedoms in the classroom, like those in the adult world, are justified, when they are so, by their results in practice.

What is true of the pupil's freedoms is true also of the teacher's. A teacher must have some freedoms in order to teach at all. The question is: how far should a teacher be free to teach as he pleases and what he pleases? What, if any, should be the limits to his freedom in respect of the methods he uses and the curriculum he implements? Once again the truth is that a teacher's freedoms are justified, in so far as they are, by the extent to which they genuinely serve the end of education. If it can be shown that a given freedom results in well-taught, interested pupils, then the freedom is to that extent justified; if not, then the freedom is at least suspect. Much the same might be said about the teacher's freedoms outside the classroom. In the past, the schoolteacher, like the clergyman, tended to be regarded by the public at large as what Samuel Butler called a sort of human Sunday, one whose general behaviour was far more circumscribed than was the case with other people. A permissive social climate has to a large extent weakened this assumption, if not for clergymen, certainly for teachers who have to a very large extent emancipated themselves from the stricter conventions which governed their out-of-school behaviour earlier this century. The emancipation has not been complete, however, and there are still those who hold that the teacher's special role in society demands that his range of social freedoms, those concerned with industrial action, political protest and sexual behaviour, for example, should be to some extent limited. This question is by no means settled. The difficulty lies in determining just how far the exercise of adult, out-of-school freedoms affects the teacher's influence as an exemplar to the young people to whom he has a special responsibility.

## 4 Democracy and education

We come now to the theory that education ought to be closely allied to the practice and institutions of democracy, that the aim of education should be the production of 'democratic' man, and that education should be 'democratic'. Here again we are in some difficulty since the term 'democracy' is capable of so many interpretations as to drain it of any descriptive precision. The term originated as a description of a particular form of government, government by the 'many', but it has now broadened in meaning so as to cover almost any kind of social levelling or any kind of group participation in events or decisions. As with 'equality' and 'freedom', it carries strong overtones of commendation. Any political group with serious aspirations to power must declare its commitment to 'democracy', and to call any institution, practice or proceeding 'democratic' is to register approval of it. This is, unfortunately, quite compatible with the fact that democratic decisions and practices may be unjust, inept and sometimes disastrous. Plato, who feared what democracy might do, and with an eye on what democracy had done in his time, thought it a very bad form of government and threw his considerable intellectual weight against it.

Democracy, however, has no doubt come to stay, and in our contemporary society there is a persistent call for education to be 'democratic'. This call may be variously interpreted. It may indicate or articulate a general theory of education, to the effect that education should serve the purposes of democracy by producing citizens able and willing to maintain a democratic society. It

129

may indicate a mixed pedagogical and social theory, namely, that schools and other educational institutions should themselves be organised on democratic lines. Or it may be the expression of the theory that education should be in some sense 'accountable' to the society that provides it. We may note that these are three prescriptive theories concerning education and as such provide opportunities for philosophical scrutiny of their purport and acceptability.

The first, the general theory that education should serve democracy by producing democrats, seems irreproachable given the initial assumption that a democratic society is desirable. A democratic society involves an appeal to individual members on matters of social concern, and depends on the working of a complex of institutions, public discussions, voting, representative bodies, majority decisions and the like. Along with these institutional features goes, ideally, a willingness to work the system, to allow free expression of opinion, to abide by majority decisions, to participate in the various procedures. Without a general adherence to these principles and practices a democracy would not long survive. Democratic society depends on democratic man. So, it has been argued, it is in the public interest for a democracy to provide an education in democracy for its future citizens. [27] This would involve some kind of political education, an initiation into the practice of group decision-making and the inculcation of a commitment to such principles as the adherence to majority decisions, toleration of differing opinions, and an introduction to the institutional structure of democratic society. Those who hold this view often advocate this sort of education for children in school. Two points might be made about this. Firstly, the argument that it is in the public interest for a democracy to provide an education in democracy begs an important question. Plainly, if it is in the public interest for society to be democratic, it will be in the public interest to provide whatever is necessary, education included, to sustain a democracy. The same could be said for any form of social polity whatever. If it were in the public interest to maintain a fascist or a communist society it would be in the public interest to provide a fascist or a communist type of education. But the important prior question must be: is it in the public interest that the society should be fascist, or communist, or democratic? Attention must be directed to the major assumption in each case. A democratic education is only in the public interest if democracy is so. The assumption that it is needs to be justified rather than stipulated, and, it should be said, the justification requires more than a writing-in to the term 'democracy' such virtues as justice, freedom and toleration. A democracy need have none of those virtues. The second point is that, granted the need for a democratic sort of education, it is an arguable matter whether or not this is appropriate for schools to give or children to receive. The assumption that because education in democracy is desirable schools should provide it for children is quite gratuitous. It may be that given the relatively short time children spend in school and the demands already made on them there, there are more urgent things to be learned at school than the elements of democratic politics. It may be that political education is best acquired in practice and in adult life.

131

The second, more limited theory is that schools and other educational establishments should themselves be run on 'democratic' lines. This theory has links with the first, indeed it forms part of the 'methods' assumption of the general theory. It is assumed that actual democracy in school would supply the practical element in an education for democracy. But it is also advocated on grounds of justice, that pupils and students have a 'right' to take part in the running of these institutions.

This contention raises the important issue of the substantial forms of democracy. Present-day democracies tend to be of one of two main kinds. The first is that which exists mainly in Western Europe, North America and Australasia, and is often called a 'liberal' democracy. Here, in its simplest terms, the model is as follows: everyone over a certain age is entitled to express his political opinions and to register these opinions by means of a vote at elections. The elections enable a government to be formed. Governments, since they rest on election, are ultimately responsive to the opinions of the electorate and will resign when majority opinion goes against them. In office, government will generally try to act in ways compatible with what it regards as the best interests of the people, but if there is a serious conflict between the people's interests as seen by the government and the people's declared opinions, the government will at last give way to opinion. No matter how foolish the government may think the electorate's opinions are, nor how obviously those opinions really go against their true interests, the government will, if it comes to a collision, respond to the people's opinions, amending or even abandoning policies, or, if required, resigning as a government.

The other kind of democracy, sometimes called a 'people's democracy' is found mainly in Eastern Europe and the USSR. Here we have the institutional apparatus of a liberal democracy, votes, elections, assemblies, but with a significant difference. In a 'people's democracy' it is not the people's opinions which are ultimately to prevail, but rather what the government considers to be the 'real' interests of the people. The governments of such democracies do not resign when opinions go against them. They take their stand on the people's interests, and if these conflict with popular opinions it is the opinions which are, so far as possible, set aside. Governments usually manage this by making sure that unwelcome opinions do not circulate widely, and by arranging elections so that there is no question of the government not being elected. It is only when opinions are organised to the point of exerting non-political force that the government is likely to make major concessions to opinion, as in Poland in 1980. Short of this it is the government's view of the 'real' interests of the people that carries the day. It is paradoxical but true to say that whilst liberal democracies really are 'people's' democracies, the so-called 'people's democracies' are not so. They are at best paternalistic governments, going along with popular opinion so far as they can, but ultimately and essentially concerned with what they consider to be the real interests of the governed.

The interesting question now is: supposing there to be a case for democracy in schools, which of these two versions of democracy is the more appropriate? One would be pleased to be able to say: the liberal version, the model we adopt ourselves in adult society. But here we have a difficulty. In schools we are dealing with children, and it is the business of schools to educate children, which means consulting and furthering their long-term interests as growing human beings. Children and young people will have opinions, likes and dislikes, but these will not always, perhaps not often, coincide with their real interests. Children do not always see clearly what is good for them, and teachers quite often have to oppose children's whims and fancies with considerations of their real welfare. Now, let us suppose that we are committed to running a school as a democracy, with institutions which register children's opinions, by votes, elections, majority decisions and so on. If we genuinely adhere to the liberal model the authority structure of the school would have to be responsive to these declared opinions, which might, and frequently would, run counter to what is in the children's interests. At this point democracy would be anti-educational. From which it would seem to follow that a liberal version of democracy is not really appropriate in schools, and children, in so far as they are in pupillage, have no real 'rights' in the matter of running the institution which cares for them. It is their long-term interests which are of first importance, not their 'rights' as political members, since they are not political members at all.

The form of democracy appropriate for schools, supposing any to be so, would be the paternalistic kind, one which maintained the institutional apparatus of democracy, which acceded to pupil's opinion so far as possible, but where, ultimately, the teaching staff would have to set aside opinions where their implementation in practice would be against the children's interests. Headmasters who recognise this rather obvious point and who run a more or less paternalistic form of democracy in their schools are often criticised for practising a 'sham' democracy. Such criticism is misguided and unfair. This is the only kind of democracy appropriate for schools if schools are to be instruments of education. It is the kind of democracy which allows children to participate in democratic procedures under conditions in which they can do themselves little harm. It is a preparation for democracy of the liberal kind, although it falls short of this version of democracy. An objection to the paternalistic 'people's democracies' is that they treat adults as children, subordinating their opinions to what is thought to be their interests. This is no objection to the adoption of this model in schools where the 'electorate' *are* children. Of course, in those institutions where the electorate are students rather than pupils, the case for a liberal type of democracy is much stronger, but even here democracy should give way to education if the two conflict. One possible area of such conflict would be between students' opinions and the considered judgment of the teacher as authority on his subject. In this case the only appropriate deciding factor would be a consideration of truth, not an aggregation of votes.

The third theory, that education should be democratic in the sense of being accountable to society, to 'the people', is really a theory of an extra-educational kind, belonging perhaps to political or social theory. There is a distinction to be made here. Discussions about what it might mean to say that there should be equality in education, or that education should be along the lines of freedom, or be 'democratic' in practice, refer to what can be, or should be, done by those working *within* education, as a matter of method or practice. Discussions of the 'accountability' kind refer mainly to relationships between internal educational practice and outside influences, like governments, employers, churches and parents. They raise interesting questions, particularly in the area of curriculum content, about who should say what goes into the curriculum and who should decide what educational methods should be used. These are questions which require a fuller treatment than is possible here.

## 5 Conclusion

This chapter deals with three major theories about educational practice which spring from the social aspect of education. The theories were: that education should distribute its goods and advantages equally amongst those it deals with; that education should be conducted under conditions of freedom, both for pupils and for their teachers; and finally, that education should aim at producing citizens for a democracy and that, as a means to that end, schools themselves should be democratic institutions. In each case there was an attempt to deal with the theory as a theory, to bring out as clearly as possible what was being prescribed and then to examine its justification, its claim to acceptability. The conclusions arrived at were: that the concern for educational equality would be better expressed as a concern for justice, and that the implementation of justice in education is compatible with a variety of different educational provisions; that some freedoms are prerequisites of education but that particular freedoms must be judged by their educational consequences; that democratic education is desirable to the extent to which democracy itself is a desirable political arrangement, and that the practice of democracy in schools must be limited by the purpose for which schools exist: the education of children and a concern for their long-term welfare.

## Suggestions for further reading

Each topic treated in this chapter has produced a more or less inexhaustible general literature and their application to education provides a continuing source of debate and controversy amongst philosophers. The concepts of equality, freedom and democracy and their relevance to education are treated clearly and authoritatively in R.S. Peters, *Ethics and Education*. R. Barrow deals with freedom and equality in the context of Plato's theory of education in *Plato, Utilitarianism and Education* (Routledge & Kegan Paul, 1975). An interesting paper on the relationship between education and democracy is 'Education, Democracy and the Public Interest' by P.A. White in *The Philosophy of Education*, ed. R.S. Peters (Oxford University Press, 1973).

# Bibliography

[1] AYER, A.J., *The Problem of Knowledge* (Penguin, 1956).

[2] DEWEY, J., *Democracy and Education* (New York: Macmillan, 1916).

[3] DEWEY, J., *Experience and Education* (New York: Macmillan, 1938).

[4] DURKHEIM, E., *Education and Sociology* (Chicago: Free Press, 1956).

[5] FROEBEL, F., *The Education of Man* (Fairfield, New Jersey: Kelley, 1900).

[6] HIRST, P.H., *Knowledge and the Curriculum* (Routledge & Kegan Paul, 1974).

[7] HIRST, P.H. and PETERS, R.S., *The Logic of Education* (Routledge & Kegan Paul, 1970).

[8] HOBBES, T., *Leviathan* (Collier-Macmillan, 1963).

[9] HUME, D., *An Enquiry Concerning Human Understanding* (La Salle: Open Court, 1977).

[10] KANT, I., *Critique of Pure Reason* (Dent, 1969).

[11] MILL, J., 'Essay on Education' in *James Mill on Education*, W. H. Burston (Cambridge University Press, 1969).

[12] MOORE, T.W. *Educational Theory: An Introduction* (Routledge & Kegan Paul, 1974).

[13] MOORE, T.W., 'Punishment and Education', *Proceedings of the Philosophy of Education Society of Great Britain*, 1966.

*Bibliography*

[14] NEWMAN, J.H., *On the Scope and Nature of University Education* (Dent, 1915).

[15] OAKESHOTT, M., 'Education: The Engagement and its Frustration', in *Education and the Development of Reason*, eds Dearden, Hirst and Peters, (Routledge & Kegan Paul, 1972).

[16] PETERS, R.S., *Ethics and Education* (Allen & Unwin, 1966).

[17] PETERS, R.S., *Essays on Educators* (Allen & Unwin, 1981).

[18] PIAGET, J., *The Moral Judgment of the Child* (Routledge & Kegan Paul, 1932).

[19] PLATO, *The Republic* (Penguin, 1970).

[20] QUINTON, A., *Utilitarian Ethics* (Macmillan, 1973).

[21] ROUSSEAU, J.J., *Emile* (Dent, 1974).

[22] RYLE, G., *The Concept of Mind* (Penguin, 1963).

[23] SCHEFFLER, I., *The Language of Education* (Charles C. Thomas, 1962).

[24] SNOOK, I.A., *Indoctrination and Education* (Routledge & Kegan Paul, 1972).

[25] SPENCER, H., *Education* (Dent, 1911).

[26] SKINNER, B.F., *Walden Two* (New York: Macmillan, 1953).

[27] WHITE, P.A., 'Democracy and the Public Interest', in *The Philosophy of Education, Oxford Readings in Philosophy*, ed. R.S. Peters (Oxford University Press, 1973).

[28] YOUNG, M. (ed.), *Knowledge and Control* (Collier-Macmillan, 1971).

# Index

### Philosophy of Education: An Introduction

T. W. Moore here provides an introduction to the philosophy of education, which will enable students meeting the subject for the first time to find their way among the many specialized volumes. It deals in a non-technical way with the more important issues raised in a philosophical approach to education, and gives a clear idea of the scope of the subject.

After discussing different theories of the aims of education, whether mechanistic or organic, Mr Moore passes on to practical issues — for example, about the curriculum, the distinction between education and indoctrination, the rôle of authority and discipline, and the place of religious and moral teaching. Finally, he deals with some important aspects of education and the influence of different political structures on the philosophy of education. Suggestions for further reading are given for each chapter.

Professor R. S. Peters, in the General Editor's Note, writes: 'This concise introduction to philosophy of education is readable, succinct and informative. It should be of great help to teachers, and anyone interested in philosophy of education, to find their way into the considerable literature that now exists in this branch of educational studies.'

The Author

T. W. Moore is a Senior Lecturer in Philosophy of Education at the University of London Institute of Education. He has taught in primary and secondary schools and has been a lecturer in colleges of education. He is the author of *Educational Theory: An Introduction* (Routledge & Kegan Paul, 1974).

ISBN 0-7100-9192-3

9 780710 091925

£5.95 net